Raspberry Pi

**Tag Recognition, XBee Module, Continuous
Face Recognition, Interfacing MCP4725 12-
Bit DAC, Manufacture your own Google,
Set Up a Minecraft Server etc..,**

ANBAZHAGAN K

ACKNOWLEDGMENTS

The writer might want to recognize the diligent work of the article group in assembling this book. He might likewise want to recognize the diligent work of the Raspberry Pi Foundation and the Arduino bunch for assembling items and networks that help to make the Internet of Things increasingly open to the overall population. Yahoo for the democratization of innovation!

INTRODUCTION

The Internet of Things (IOT) is a perplexing idea comprised of numerous PCs and numerous correspondence ways. Some IOT gadgets are associated with the Internet and some are most certainly not. Some IOT gadgets structure swarms that convey among themselves. Some are intended for a solitary reason, while some are increasingly universally useful PCs. This book is intended to demonstrate to you the IOT from the back to front. By structure IOT gadgets, the per user will comprehend the essential ideas and will almost certainly develop utilizing the rudiments to make his or her very own IOT applications. These included ventures will tell the per user the best way to assemble their very own IOT ventures and to develop the models appeared. The significance of Computer Security in IOT gadgets is additionally talked about and different systems for protecting the IOT from unapproved clients or programmers. The most significant takeaway from this book is in structure the tasks yourself.

1. TAG RECOGNITION UTILIZING RASPBERRY PI AS WELL AS OPENCV

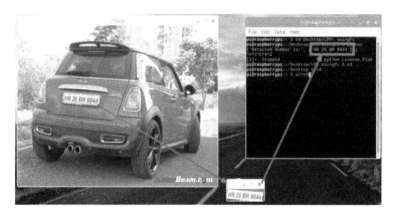

Security has consistently been a significant worry for humanity. Today we have video reconnaissance cameras in schools, medical clinics and each other open spot to make us feel verified. As indicated by a study by HIS it is evaluated that there were around 245 million surveillance cameras introduced and working back on 2014, which resembles having one surveillance camera for each 30 individuals on this planet. With the headway in innovation particularly in Image preparing and Machine Learning, it is conceivable to make these cameras more brilliant via preparing them to process data from the Video feed.

The video feed from these cameras can be used to perform face acknowledgment, design investigation, feeling examination and substantially more which would truly get it near something like the "God's Eye" appeared in the FF7 film. Truth be told, reconnaissance organizations like Hikvision and numerous others have just begun executing these highlights in their items. We recently utilized MATLAB Image handling to peruse the number plate, today in this article we will figure out how to perceive and peruse License Plate Number from Automobiles utilizing Raspberry Pi and OpenCV. We will utilize some arbitrary vehicle pictures from Google and compose a program to perceive the number plate utilizing OpenCV Contour Detection and afterward read the number from the plate utilizing Tesseract OCR. Sounds fascinating right!, so Let's begin.

Pre-requisites

As told before we will utilize the OpenCV Library to distinguish and perceive faces. So make a point to introduce OpenCV Library on Raspberry Pi before continuing with this instructional exercise. Likewise Power your Pi with a 2A connector as well as combine it to a presentation screen for simpler investigating.

This instructional exercise won't clarify how precisely OpenCV functions, in case you are interested on learning Image preparing, at that point look at this OpenCV essentials and propelled Image handling instructional exercises. You can likewise find out about forms, Blob Detection and so forth in this Image Segmentation instructional exercise utilizing OpenCV. We will plan something comparative for this to distinguish the tag of the vehicle from the picture.

Steps involved in License Plate Recognition using Raspberry Pi

Tag Recognition or LPR for short, includes three significant advances. The means are as per the following

1. Tag Detection: The initial step is to identify the License plate from the vehicle. We will utilize the form choice in OpenCV to recognize for rectangular articles to locate the number plate. The exactness can be improved in case we know the definite size, shading and estimated area of the number plate. Ordinarily the recognition calculation is prepared dependent on the situation of camera and sort of number plate utilized in that specific nation. This gets trickier if the picture doesn't have a vehicle, for this situation we will an extra advance to identify the vehicle and afterward the tag.

2. Character Segmentation: Once we have recognized the License Plate we need to trim it out and spare it as another picture. Again this should be possible effectively utilizing OpenCV.

3. Character Recognition: Now, the new picture that we acquired in the past advance makes certain to have a few characters (Numbers/Alphabets) composed on it. Along these lines, we can perform OCR (Optical Character Recognition) on it to identify the number. We previously clarified Optical Character Recognition utilizing Raspberry Pi.

1. License Plate Detection

The initial phase in this Raspberry Pi License Plate Reader is to distinguish the License Plate. We should take an example picture of a vehicle as well as start with recognizing the License Plate on that vehicle.

We will at that point utilize a similar picture for Character Segmentation and Character Recognition also. On the off chance that you need to bounce straight into the code without clarification, at that point you can look down to the base of this page, where the total code is given. The test picture that I am utilizing for this instructional exercise is demonstrated as follows.

Stage 1: Resize the picture to the necessary size and afterward grayscale it. The code for the equivalent is given beneath

```
img = cv2.resize(img, (620,480) )
```

> ### gray = cv2.cvtColor(img, cv2.COLOR_B-
> GR2GRAY) #convert to grey scale

Resizing we help us to keep away from any issues with greater goals pictures, ensure the number plate still stays in the edge in case of resizing. Dim scaling is normal in all picture preparing steps. This paces up other after procedure sine we never again need to manage the shading subtleties when handling a picture. The picture would be changed something like this when this progression is finished

Stage 2: Every picture will have valuable and point-

less data, for this situation for us just the tag is the helpful data the rest are practically futile for our program. This futile data is called commotion. Regularly utilizing a reciprocal channel (Bluring) will expel the undesirable subtleties from a picture. The code for the equivalent is

gray = cv2.bilateralFilter(gray, 11, 17, 17)

Language structure is destination_image = cv2.bilateralFilter(source_image, measurement of pixel, sigmaColor, sigmaSpace). You can expand the sigma shading and sigma space from 17 to higher qualities to obscure out more foundation data, yet be cautious that the helpful part doesn't get obscured. The yield picture is demonstrated as follows, as should be obvious the foundation subtleties (tree and building) are obscured in this picture. Along these lines we can maintain a strategic distance from the program from focusing on these areas later.

Stage 3: The following stage is intriguing where we perform edge identification. There are numerous approaches to do it, the most simple and famous route is to utilize the vigilant edge technique from OpenCV. The line to do the equivalent is demonstrated as follows

edged = cv2.Canny(gray, 30, 200) #Perform Edge detection

The linguistic structure will be destination_image = cv2.Canny(source_image, thresholdValue 1, thresholdValue 2). The Threshold Vale 1 and Threshold Value 2 are the base and most extreme limit esteems.

Just the edges that have a power slope more than the base edge esteem and not exactly the greatest edge worth will be shown. The subsequent picture is demonstrated as follows

Stage 4: Now we can begin searching for forms on our picture, we have just found out about how to discover shapes utilizing OpenCV in our past instructional exercise so we simply continue like the equivalent.

```
nts   =   cv2.findContours(edged.copy(),
cv2.RETR_TREE,           cv2.CHAIN_AP-
PROX_SIMPLE)
```

```
cnts = imutils.grab_contours(cnts)

cnts = sorted(cnts, key = cv2.contourArea,
reverse = True)[:10]

screenCnt = None
```

When the counters have been distinguished we sort them from enormous to little and consider just the initial 10 outcomes disregarding the others. In our picture the counter could be whatever has a shut surface however of all the acquired outcomes the tag number will likewise be there since it is additionally a shut surface.

To channel the tag picture among the got outcomes, we will circle however every one of the outcomes and check which has a square shape form with four sides and shut figure. Since a tag would be a square shape four sided figure.

```
# loop over our contours

for c in cnts:

        # approximate the contour

        peri = cv2.arcLength(c, True)
```

```
approx   =   cv2.approxPolyDP(c,
0.018 * peri, True)

    # if our approximated contour has
four points, then

    # we can assume that we have
found our screen

    if len(approx) == 4:

        screenCnt = approx

        break
```

The worth 0.018 is a trial esteem; you can play around it to check which works best for you. Or in case take it to next level by utilizing AI to prepare dependent on vehicle pictures and afterward utilize the correct an incentive there. When we have discovered the correct counter we spare it in a variable called screenCnt and afterward draw a square shape box around it to ensure we have distinguished the tag accurately.

Stage 5: Now that we know where the number plate is, the rest of the data is practically pointless for us. So we can continue with covering the whole picture aside from where the number plate is. The code to do the equivalent is demonstrated as follows

 # Masking the part other than the number plate

mask = np.zeros(gray.shape,np.uint8)

new_image = cv2.drawContours(mask,

[screenCnt],0,255,-1,)

new_image = cv2.bitwise_and(img,img, mask=mask)

The veiled new picture will show up something like beneath

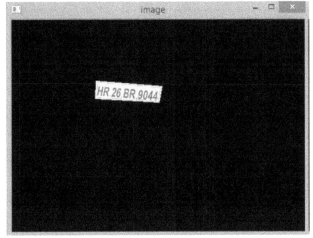

2. Character Segmentation

The subsequent stage in Raspberry Pi Number Plate Recognition is to fragment the tag out of the picture by trimming it and sparing it as another picture. We would then be able to utilize this picture to distinguish the character in it. The code to trim the return for money invested (Region of premium) picture structure the fundamental picture is demonstrated as follows

```
# Now crop

(x, y) = np.where(mask == 255)

(topx, topy) = (np.min(x), np.min(y))

(bottomx, bottomy) = (np.max(x), np.max(y))

Cropped = gray[topx:bottomx+1, topy:bottomy+1]
```

The subsequent picture is demonstrated as follows. Regularly added to trimming the picture, we can likewise dim it and edge it whenever required. This is done to improve the character acknowledgment in subsequent stage. Anyway I found that it works fine even with the first picture.

3. Character Recognition

The Final advance in this Raspberry Pi Number Plate Recognition is to really peruse the number plate data from the divided picture. We will utilize the pytesseract bundle to peruse characters from picture, much the same as we did in past instructional exercise. The code for the equivalent is given underneath

---

#Read the number plate

text = pytesseract.image_to_string(Cropped, config='--psm 11')

print("Detected Number is:",text)

We have just disclosed how to arrange a Tesseract motor, so here again if necessary we can design the Tesseract OCR to get better outcomes whenever required. The recognized character is then imprinted on the comfort. When incorporated the outcome is appeared as underneath

As should be obvious the first picture had the number "HR 25 BR9044" on it and our program has identified it printed a similar incentive on screen.

Fail Cases in Number Plate Recognition

The total undertaking document this Raspberry Pi License Plate Recognition can be downloaded from here, it contains the program and the test pictures that we used to check our program. Without being stated, it is to be recalled that the outcomes from this strategy won't be exact. The exactness relies upon the clearness of picture, direction, light presentation and so forth. To show signs of improvement results you can have a go at actualizing Machine learning calculations alongside this.

To get a thought, we should take a gander at another model where the vehicle isn't confronting the camera legitimately.

As should be obvious, our program had the option to recognize the tag accurately and crop it. In any case, the Tesseract library has neglected to perceive the characters appropriately. Rather than the real "TS 08 UE 3396" the OCR has remembered it to be "1508 ye 3396". Issues like this can be revised by either utilizing better direction pictures or by designing the Tesseract motor.

Another most dire outcome imaginable is the place the form neglects to identify the tag effectively. The underneath picture has a lot of foundation data and terrible lighting that the program has even neglected to distinguish the tag from the number. For this situation we need to again transfer on Machine learning or improve the nature of the image.

Other Successful Examples

The majority of the hours of the picture quality and direction is right, the program had the option to recognize the tag and peruse the number from it. The underneath depictions show not many of the victories acquired. Again all the test pictures and the code utilized here will be accessible in the ZIP record gave here.

Expectation you comprehended Automatic Number Plate Recognition utilizing Raspberry Pi and delighted in building something cool without anyone else. What else do you think should be possible with OpenCV and Tesseract?,

Code

```
import cv2
import imutils
import numpy as np
import pytesseract
from PIL import Image
img    =    cv2.imread('4.jpg',cv2.IMREAD_
COLOR)
img = cv2.resize(img, (620,480) )
gray = cv2.cvtColor(img, cv2.COLOR_BGR2G-
RAY) #convert to grey scale
gray    =    cv2.bilateralFilter(gray, 11, 17, 17)
#Blur to reduce noise
edged = cv2.Canny(gray, 30, 200) #Perform
Edge detection
# find contours in the edged image, keep only
the largest
# ones, and initialize our screen contour
cnts    =    cv2.findContours(edged.copy(),
cv2.RETR_TREE, cv2.CHAIN_APPROX_SIM-
PLE)
cnts = imutils.grab_contours(cnts)
```

```
cnts = sorted(cnts, key = cv2.contourArea,
reverse = True)[:10]
screenCnt = None
# loop over our contours
for c in cnts:
 # approximate the contour
 peri = cv2.arcLength(c, True)
 approx = cv2.approxPolyDP(c, 0.018 * peri,
True)


 # if our approximated contour has four
points, then
 # we can assume that we have found our
screen
 if len(approx) == 4:
  screenCnt = approx
  break
if screenCnt is None:
 detected = 0
 print "No contour detected"
else:
 detected = 1
if detected == 1:
 cv2.drawContours(img, [screenCnt], -1, (0,
255, 0), 3)
# Masking the part other than the number
```

```
plate
mask = np.zeros(gray.shape,np.uint8)
new_image    =    cv2.drawContours(mask,
[screenCnt],0,255,-1,)
new_image    =    cv2.bitwise_and(img,img,
mask=mask)
# Now crop
(x, y) = np.where(mask == 255)
(topx, topy) = (np.min(x), np.min(y))
(bottomx,    bottomy)    =    (np.max(x),
np.max(y))
Cropped = gray[topx:bottomx+1, topy:bot-
tomy+1]
#Read the number plate
text = pytesseract.image_to_string(Cropped,
config='--psm 11')
print("Detected Number is:",text)
cv2.imshow('image',img)
cv2.imshow('Cropped',Cropped)
cv2.waitKey(0)
cv2.destroyAllWindows()
```

2. THE MOST EFFECTIVE METHOD TO INTERFACE XBEE MODULE WITH RASPBERRY PI

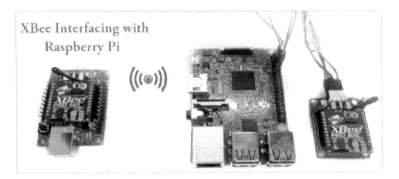

In past instructional exercise we interfaced the XBee module with Arduino Uno as well as caused them to convey remotely utilizing XBee module. Presently we will interface XBee module with Raspberry Pi which will go about as a beneficiary and cause it to discuss remotely with another XBee module (XBee pioneer board) which is sequentially associated with the workstation.

Hardware Requirements

- 1 x Raspberry Pi with Raspbian Installed in it

- 1 x XBee traveler board (discretionary)

- 2 x XBee Pro S2C modules (some other model can be utilized)

- USB links

- 1 x Xbee Breakout board (discretionary)

- LEDs

It is accepted that your Raspberry Pi is as of now flashed with a working framework. If not, pursue the

Getting started with Raspberry Pi instructional exercise before continuing. Here we are utilizing Rasbian Jessie introduced Raspberry Pi 3.

Here External Monitor utilizing HDMI link is utilized as show to interface with Raspberry Pi. In case you don't have screen, you can utilize SSH customer (Putty) or VNC server to associate with Raspberry pi utilizing Laptop or PC. Become familiar with setting up Raspberry Pi headlessly here.

Configuring XBee Modules using XCTU

As we have learnt in past instructional exercise of ZigBee Introduction that the XBee module can go about as a Coordinator, Router or an End gadget yet it should be designed to work in wanted mode. Thus, before utilizing the XBee modules with Raspberry Pi, we need to arrange these modules utilizing XCTU programming.

To interface XBee module with the PC, a USB to sequential converter or explicitly structured adventurer board is utilized. Simply connect the XBee module to the Explorer board and fitting it with the PC utilizing USB link.

In the event that you don't have any converter or wayfarer board, at that point an Arduino board can be utilized as a USB to sequential gadget which can undoubtedly speak with the XBee and PC. Simply transfer clear sketch in Arduino board and now it can act like a USB to Serial converter.

Designing XBee Modules:

Here in this instructional exercise, an Explorer board is utilized to design the XBee modules.

Download the XCTU programming from this connection and introduce it. Subsequent to downloading and introducing the XCTU programming, open it and ensure your XBee module is appropriately associated. Check the COM port of the Arduino board in gadget chief.

1. Presently, click on the hunt button. This will give all of you the RF gadgets associated with your workstation. For our situation, it will show only one XBee module.

2. Select the Serial port of the Explorer board/Arduino board and snap on Next.

3. In the following window, set the USB port parameters as appeared underneath and click on Finish.

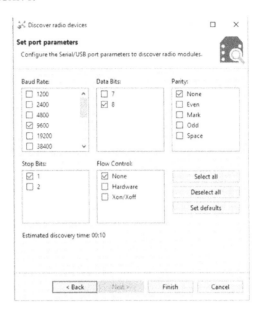

4. Select the Discovered gadget and snap on Add chosen gadget. This procedure will add your XBee module to XCTU dashboard.

5. Presently, you can design your XBee module in this window. You can utilize either AT directions or put the information physically. As should be obvious, there is R appearing on the left board which implies XBee is in switch mode. We need to make it Coordinator for the transmitter part.

To start with, update the Firmware by tapping on the Update firmware.

6. Pick the Product group of your gadget which is accessible on back of your XBee module. Select capacity set and firmware form as featured beneath and click on Update.

7. Presently, you need to give ID, MY and DL information to make association with other XBee. ID stays same for both the modules. Just MY and DL informa-

tion exchange for example MY for the recipient XBee becomes DL of the transmitter XBee (facilitator) and DL for the collector XBee turns into MY of the transmitter XBee. Make CE as Coordinator and afterward hit the Write button. As demonstrated as follows.

	ATMY	*ATID*	*ATID*
XBee 1 coordinator	*1234*	*5678*	*2244*
XBee 2 end device	*5678*	*1234*	*2244*

8. In the wake of composing the above information to the transmitter part, plug out it from the adventurer board and fitting in the second XBee module in it. Rehash a similar procedure as above just changes are the DL, MY, and CE. As we will cause the second To xbee as End gadget so in CE drop down menu, select the End

gadget and hit the Write button.

9. Presently, our XBee modules are prepared to interface with the Raspberry Pi. We will associate the transmitter XBee to the PC and recipient XBee with the Raspberry Pi. At that point offer directions to the collector part utilizing workstation. PC.
Circuit Diagram for Receiver Part

Associations for interfacing ZigBee module with Raspberry PI are appeared in the circuit chart.

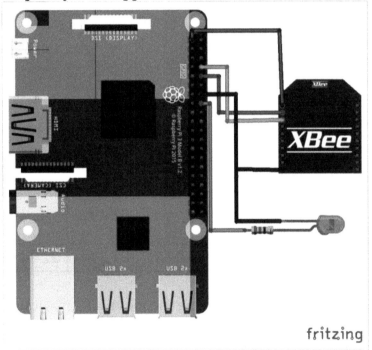

Associations:

- Tx (pin2)of XBee - > Tx of stick Raspberry Pi

- Rx(pin3) of XBee - > Rx of stick Raspberry Pi

- Gnd (pin10) of XBee - > GND of stick Raspberry Pi

- Vcc (Pin1) of XBee - > 3.3v of stick Raspberry Pi

- Driven is associated with GPIO 23

Setup Raspberry Pi for Serial communication

Presently, we will arrangement the Raspberry Pi for the Serial correspondence. As a matter of course, the equipment sequential port of Pi is crippled. Thus, we need to empower it before beginning the association.

1. In the terminal, run the order raspi-config.

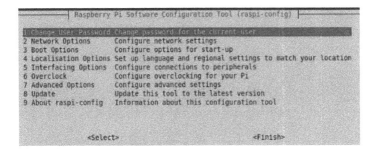

2. Go to alternative 5 Interfacing choices and hit the enter. Presently, select the P6 Serial alternative and Enable it and afterward spare.

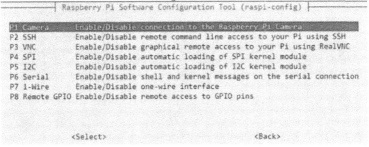

Leave the terminal as well as you are good to go to make the association between Raspberry Pi and XBee. GPIO 14 and 15 will go about as Tx and Rx individually and these are accessible at /dev/ttyS0 port of raspberry pi.

Presently, we will compose a python content to ON the LED at whatever point we get 'a' from the transmitter side XBee.

Programming Raspberry Pi for XBee communication

Complete python program for interfacing XBee with

Raspberry Pi is given toward the end.

In the first place, we need to import the time, sequential and RPi.GPIO libraries utilizing import work.

```
import time

import serial

import RPi.GPIO as GPIO

...
```

Presently, compose the properties of sequential association, characterize port, baudrate and equalities as beneath.

```
ser = serial.Serial(

    port='/dev/ttyS0',

    baudrate = 9600,

    parity=serial.PARITY_NONE,

    stopbits=serial.STOPBITS_ONE,

    bytesize=serial.EIGHTBITS,
```

```
timeout=1

)
```

Compose all the send and getting components in the while circle.

```
while 1:
```

You can utilize ser.write capacity to send the messages to the transmitter side. Uncomment the beneath lines to send countings.

```
#ser.write(str.encode('Write counter: %d
\n'%(counter)))

#time.sleep(1)

#counter += 1
```

For accepting the messages we need to utilize ser.readline() work. Store the approaching message in a variable as well as check the condition. In case that approaching message is 'an' at that point turn ON the LED for 3 seconds and afterward turn OFF the LED.

```
x=ser.readline().strip()

 print(x)

 if x == 'a':

   GPIO.output(23,GPIO.HIGH)

   time.sleep(3)

 ..

 ..
```

Complete Python code is given toward the finish of the instructional exercise. Glue the code in any content tool of the Pi and spare it. Run the content in the terminal utilizing sudo python script_name.py OR you can utilize Python IDE and Shell to execute the content.

Testing the wireless XBee communication using Raspberry Pi

Presently, we as a whole set to test our XBee transmitter and recipient. To offer direction to the transmitter part, we will utilize XCTU's support terminal. Snap on the Console symbol close to the settings alternative. At that point, click on Open catch to interface the XBee to the PC.

Enter 'an' in Console log. You will see that LED will turn ON for three seconds as well as afterward it turn OFF.

Along these lines you can likewise associate the transmitter XBee to the Arduino board as portrayed in the past instructional exercise, and make the Raspberry Pi and Arduino to speak with one another.

Code

```
#!/usr/bin/env python
import time
import serial
import RPi.GPIO as GPIO
GPIO.setmode(GPIO.BCM)
GPIO.setwarnings(False)
GPIO.setup(23,GPIO.OUT)
ser = serial.Serial(
```

```
    port='/dev/ttyS0',
    baudrate = 9600,
    parity=serial.PARITY_NONE,
    stopbits=serial.STOPBITS_ONE,
    bytesize=serial.EIGHTBITS,
    timeout=1
)
counter=0

while 1:
    #ser.write(str.encode('Write counter: %d
\n'%(counter)))
    #time.sleep(1)
    #counter += 1
    x=ser.readline().strip()
    print(x)
    if x == 'a':
        GPIO.output(23,GPIO.HIGH)
        time.sleep(3)
    else:
        GPIO.output(23,GPIO.LOW)
```

❖ ❖ ❖

3. CONTINUOUS FACE RECOGNITION WITH RASPBERRY PI AND OPENCV

Face Recognition is getting progressively mainstream and the majority of us are now utilizing it without acknowledging it. Be it a straightforward Facebook Tag proposal or Snapchat Filter or a propelled air terminal security observation, Face Recognition has just done something amazing in it. China has begun utilizing Face Recognition in schools to screen under-study's participation and practices. Retail locations have begun utilizing Face Recognition to classify their clients and segregate individuals with history of extortion. With much more changes in progress, there is no uncertainty that this innovation would be seen wherever sooner rather than later.

In this instructional exercise we will figure out how we can fabricate our very own Face Recognition framework utilizing the OpenCV Library on Raspberry Pi. The upside of introducing this framework on compact Raspberry Pi is that you can introduce it anyplace to work it as observation framework. Like all Face Recognition frameworks, the instructional exercise will include two python contents, one is a Trainer program which will examine a lot of photographs of a specific individual and make a dataset (YML File). The subsequent program is the Recognizer program which distinguishes a face and afterward utilizes this YML record to perceive the face and notice the individual name. Both the projects that we will talk about here are for Raspberry Pi (Linux), however will likewise chip away at Windows Computers with slight changes. We as of now have arrangement of Tutorials for apprentices for beginning with OpenCV, you can check all the OpenCV instructional exercises here.

Pre-requisites

As told before we will utilize the OpenCV Library to distinguish and perceive faces. So ensure you to introduce OpenCV Library on Pi before continuing with this instructional exercise. Additionally Power your Pi with a 2A connector and interface it to a showcase screen by means of HDMI link since we won't have the option to get the video yield through SSH.

Additionally I won't clarify how precisely OpenCV works,if you are keen on learning Image preparing then look at this OpenCV essentials and propelled Image handling instructional exercises. You can likewise find out about forms, Blob Detection and so forth in this Image Segmentation instructional exercise.

How Face Recognition Works with OpenCV

Before we start, comprehend that Face Detection as well as Face Recognition are two unique things. In Face Detection just the Face of an individual is identified the product will have no Clue who that Person is. In Face Recognition the product won't just identify the face however will likewise perceive the individual. Presently, it ought to be evident that we have to perform Face Detection before performing Face Recognition. It would not be feasible for me to clarify how precisely OpenCV identifies a face or some other article so far as that is concerned. In this line, in case you are interested to realize that you can pursue this Object Detection instructional exercise.

A video feed from a webcam is just a long grouping of still pictures being refreshed in a steady progression. What's more, every one of these pictures is only an assortment of pixels of various qualities set up together in its separate position. So by what means can a program distinguish a face from these pixels and further perceive the individual in it? There are a huge deal of calculations behind it and attempting to clarify them is past the extent of this article, yet since we are utilizing the OpenCV library it easy to perform face Recognition without getting further into the ideas

Face Detection using Cascade Classifiers in OpenCV

Just in the event that we can distinguish a face we will ready to remember it or recollect it. To identify an article, for example, face OpenCV utilizes something many refer to as Classifiers. These Classifiers are pre-prepared arrangement of information (XML File) which can be utilized to identify a specific article for our situation a face. You can get familiar with Face Detection Classifiers here. Aside from distinguishing Face, Classifiers can identify different items like nose, eyes, Vehicle License Plate, Smile and so on. The rundown of Case Classifiers can be downloaded from the ZIP record underneath

Classifiers for Object discovery in Python

On the other hand OpenCV additionally enables you to make your very own Classifier which can be utilized to recognize some other article in an Image via Training your Cascade Classifier. In this instructional exercise we will utilize a classifier called "haarcascade_frontalface_default.xml" which will identify the face from front position. We will see more on the only way to utilize Classifiers in the Programming area.

Installing the Required Packages

Ensure pip is introduced and afterward continue with introducing the accompanying bundles.

Introduce dlib: Dlib is a toolbox for certifiable Machine Learning and information examination applications. To introduce dlib, simply enter the accompanying order in the terminal

Pip install dlib

This ought to introduce dlib and when effective you will get a screen this way.

Introduce pad: Pillow otherwise called PIL represents Python Imaging Library which is utilized to open, control and spare pictures in various configuration. To introduce PIL utilize the accompanying order

Pip install pillow

Once introduced you will get a triumph message as

demonstrated as follows

Introduce face_recognition: The face_recognition library for python is viewed as least complex library to perceive and control faces. We will utilize this library to prepare and perceive faces. To introduce this library pursue the order

Pip install face_recognition –no –cache-dir

When introduced effectively you should see a screen like demonstrated as follows. The library is substantial and the vast majority will confront memory surpassing issues subsequently I have utilized the "- no -

store dir" code to introduce the library without sparing the reserve records.

Face Recognition Project Folder

Our Project envelope will comprise of two python program called the Face_Trainner.py and Face_Recog.py. An organizer called Face_Images which comprise test pictures of the people who must be perceived. A Classifier record called "haarcascade_frontalface_default.xml" which is utilized to distinguish faces. Lastly a coach record called "face-trainner.yml" which will be created utilizing the Face_Trainner.py program dependent on the Images present inside the Face_Images Folder. Every one of the documents in my task envelope are demonstrated as follows

Face_Images   Face_Recog.py   Face_Trainer.py   face-trainner.yml   haarcascade_frontal
face_default.xml

You can download the equivalent from here.
Setting up Face_Images directory with sample faces
The Face_Images registry appeared above ought to have sub-indexes with the name of the individual who ought to be perceived and scarcely any example pictures of them inside it. For this instructional exercise I have attempted to perceive myself (Anbu) and Elon Musk. So I have made just 2 sub-indexes with pictures like show underneath.

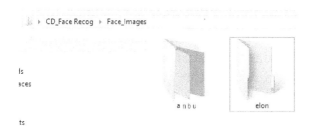

You need to rename the envelope with the name of the individual whom you are perceiving and furthermore supplant the photographs with that individual. At least 5 photographs for every individual appears to function admirably. Be that as it may, the more the quantity of people the moderate the program will be.
Face Trainer Program

How about we investigate the Face_Traineer.py program. The target of the program is to open every one of the Images in the Face_Images index and quest for faces. When the face is recognized it crops the face and changes over it to grayscale and afterward to a numpy cluster we at that point at last utilize the face_recognition library that we introduced before to prepare and spare it as a document called face-trainner.yml. The information in this record can later be utilized to perceive the appearances. The total Trainer program is given toward the end, here will clarify the most significant lines.

We start the program by bringing in the necessary modules. The cv2 module is utilized for Image Processing, the numpy is utilized to change over pictures to numerical reciprocals, os module is utilized to explore through catalogs and PIL is utilized to deal with pictures.

```
import cv2 #For Image processing

import numpy as np #For converting Images to Numerical array

import os #To handle directories

from PIL import Image #Pillow lib for handling images
```

Next we need to utilize the haarcascade_frontal-face_default.xml classifier to distinguish the countenances in pictures. Ensure you have set this xml document in your venture envelope else you will confront a blunder. At that point we utilize the recognizer variable to make a (LBPH) Face Recognizer.

```
face_cascade                              =
cv2.CascadeClassifier('haarcascade_
frontalface_default.xml')

recognizer  =  cv2.createLBPHFaceRecog-
nizer()
```

At that point we require to get into the Face_Images Directory to get to the pictures inside it. This registry ought to be set inside your present working catalog (CWD). The accompanying line is utilized to get into the envelope which is put in the CWD.

```
Face_Images  =  os.path.join(os.getcwd(),
"Face_Images") #Tell the program where
we have saved the face images
```

We at that point use for circles to get into each sub-registry of the catalog Face_Images and open any documents that end with jpeg, jpg or png. The way of each picture is put away in a variable called way and the envelope name (which will be individual's name) where the pictures are put are put away in a variable called person_name.

```
for root, dirs, files in os.walk( Face_Images): #go to the face image directory

for file in files: #check every directory in it

if file.endswith("jpeg") or file.endswith("jpg") or file.endswith("png"): #for image files ending with jpeg,jpg or png

path = os.path.join(root, file)

person_name = os.path.basename(root)
```

In the event that the name of the individual has transformed we increase a variable called Face_ID, this will help us in having distinctive Face_ID for various individual which we will later use to recognize the name of the individual.

```
if     pev_person_name!=person_name:
```

> #Check if the name of person has changed
>
> Face_ID=Face_ID+1 #If yes increment the ID count
>
> pev_person_name = person_name

As we probably am aware it is part simpler for OpenCV to work with grayscale pictures than with hued pictures since the BGR esteems can be disregarded. So to decrease the qualities in the picture we convert it to grayscale and afterward likewise resize picture to 550 with the goal that all pictures remain uniform. Ensure the face in the picture is in the center else the face will be trimmed out. At last convert every one of these pictures to numpy exhibit to get a numerical incentive for the pictures. And afterward utilize the course classifier to identify the appearances in the pictures and store the outcome in a variable called faces.

> Gery_Image = Image.open(path).convert("L") # convert the image to greysclae using Pillow
>
> Crop_Image = Gery_Image.resize((550,550) , Image.ANTIALIAS) #Crop the Grey Image to 550*550 (Make sure your

face is in the center in all image)

```
Final_Image = np.array(Crop_Image,
"uint8")
```

```
faces = face_cascade.detectMultiScale(
Final_Image, scaleFactor=1.5, minNeigh-
bors=5) #Detect The face in all sample
image
```

When the face has been recognized we will trim that territory and think about it as our Region of Interest (ROI). The ROI area will be utilized to prepare the face recognizer. We need to add each rous face inside a variable called x_train. At that line we furnish this ROI esteems alongside the Face ID incentive to the recognizer which will give us the preparation information. The information in this way acquired will be spared

```
for (x,y,w,h) in faces:
```

```
roi = Final_Image[y:y+h, x:x+w] #crop the
Region of Interest (ROI)
```

```
x_train.append(roi)
```

```
y_ID.append(Face_ID)
```

recognizer.train(x_train,   np.array(y_ID)) #Create a Matrix of Training data

recognizer.save("face-trainner.yml") #Save the matrix as YML file

At the point when you arrange this program you will find that the face-trainner.yml record gets refreshed unfailingly. So make a point to incorporate this program at whatever point you roll out any improvements to the photographs in the Face_Images index. When aggregated you will get the Face ID, way name, individual name, and numpy cluster printed like appeared underneath for investigating reason.

Face Recognizing Program

Since we have our prepared information prepared, we can utilize it to perceive faces now. In the Face Recognizer program we will get a live video feed from a USB webcam as well as afterward convert it to picture. At that point we need to utilize our face discovery strategy to distinguish for faces in those photographs and afterward contrast it and all the Face ID that we have made before. On the off chance that we discover a match we can, at that point box the face and compose the name of the individual who has been perceived. The total program is again given toward the end, the clarification for the equivalent is as per the following.

The program imparts a great deal of similitude to the coach program, so import similar modules that we utilized before and furthermore utilize the classifier since we have to perform face recognition once more.

import cv2 #For Image processing

import numpy as np #For converting Images to Numerical array

import os #To handle directories

from PIL import Image #Pillow lib for handling images

```
face_cascade                              =
cv2.CascadeClassifier('haarcascade_
frontalface_default.xml')

recognizer = cv2.createLBPHFaceRecog-
nizer()
```

Next in the variable marks, you need to compose the name of the people that were referenced in the envelope. Ensure you pursue a similar request. For my situation it is my name "Anbu" and "Elon".

```
labels = ["Anbu", "Elon Musk"]
```

We at that point need to stack the face-trainner.yml document into our program since we should utilize the information from that record to perceive faces.

```
recognizer.load("face-trainner.yml")
```

The video feed is gotten from the USB webcam. On the off chance that you have more than one camera associated supplant 0 with 1 to get to the optional camera.

```
cap = cv2.VideoCapture(0) #Get vidoe feed
from the Camera
```

Next, we break the video into outlines (Images) and convert it into grayscale and afterward distinguish the appearances in the picture. When the appearances have been distinguished we need to trim that zone simply as we did before and spare it independently as roi_gray.

```
ret, img = cap.read() # Break video into
frames

gray = cv2.cvtColor(img, cv2.COLOR_B-
GR2GRAY) #convert Video frame to Grey-
scale

faces = face_cascade.detectMultiScale(g-
ray,   scaleFactor=1.5,   minNeighbors=5)
#Recog. faces

for (x, y, w, h) in faces:

roi_gray = gray[y:y+h, x:x+w] #Convert
Face to greyscale
```

```
id_, conf = recognizer.predict(roi_gray)
#recognize the Face
```

The variable conf reveals to us how certain the product is perceiving the face. In case the certainty level is more noteworthy than 80, we get the name of the individual utilizing the ID number utilizing the beneath line of code. At that point draw a container around the substance of the individual and compose the name of the individual over the case.

```
if conf>=80:

    font = cv2.FONT_HERSHEY_SIMPLEX
#Font style for the name

    name = labels[id_] #Get the name from
the List using ID number

    cv2.putText(img, name, (x,y), font, 1,
(0,0,255), 2)

cv2.rectangle(img,(x,y),(x+w,y+h),
(0,255,0),2)
```

At long last we need to show the video feed that we simply examined and afterward break the feed when a hold up key (here q) is squeezed.

```
cv2.imshow('Preview',img) #Display the
Video

if cv2.waitKey(20) & 0xFF == ord('q'):

  break
```

Ensure the Pi is associated with a screen through HDMI when this program is executed. Run the program as well as you will discover a window springing up with name review and your video feed in it. In the event that a face is perceived in the video feed you will discover a crate around it and if your program could perceive the face it will likewise show the name of the individual. We have prepared our program to perceive myself and Elon Musk and you can see both getting perceived in the beneath preview.

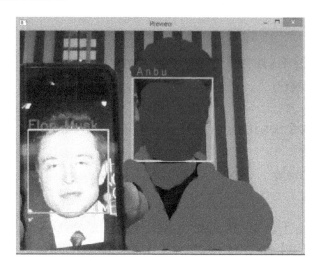

When perceptible issue is that the casing rate is extremely moderate. I am getting like one edge for like clockwork. A similar program when executed on my PC (with slight changes) gave me extremely great outcomes. Likewise don't anticipate that it should be exact, our mentor information is extremely basic so the program won't be truly solid. You can check how to utilize Deep figuring out how to prepare your dataset to improve exactness. There are approaches to build FPS (Frame every second) except let us leave that for another instructional exercise.

Expectation you comprehended the article and had the option to actualize your own face acknowledgment framework.

Code

Real Time Face Recognition Program

```
#Program to Detect the Face and Recognise
the Person based on the data from face-train-
ner.yml
import cv2 #For Image processing
import numpy as np #For converting Images
to Numerical array
import os #To handle directories
from PIL import Image #Pillow lib for hand-
ling images
labels = ["Anbu", "Elon Musk"]
face_cascade = cv2.CascadeClassifier('haar-
cascade_frontalface_default.xml')
recognizer = cv2.createLBPHFaceRecog-
nizer()
recognizer.load("face-trainner.yml")
cap = cv2.VideoCapture(0) #Get vidoe feed
from the Camera
while(True):
    ret, img = cap.read() # Break video into
frames
    gray = cv2.cvtColor(img, cv2.COLOR_B-
GR2GRAY) #convert Video frame to Greyscale
    faces = face_cascade.detectMultiScale(gray,
scaleFactor=1.5, minNeighbors=5) #Recog.
faces
    for (x, y, w, h) in faces:
```

```
    roi_gray = gray[y:y+h, x:x+w] #Convert
Face to greyscale
    id_, conf = recognizer.predict(roi_gray)
#recognize the Face
  if conf>=80:
      font = cv2.FONT_HERSHEY_SIMPLEX
#Font style for the name
  name = labels[id_] #Get the name from the
List using ID number
    cv2.putText(img, name, (x,y), font, 1,
(0,0,255), 2)
        cv2.rectangle(img,(x,y),(x+w,y+h),
(0,255,0),2)
    cv2.imshow('Preview',img) #Display the
Video
  if cv2.waitKey(20) & 0xFF == ord('q'):
  break
# When everything done, release the capture
cap.release()
cv2.destroyAllWindows()
```

Face Detection Trainer Program

```
#Program to train with the faces and create a
YAML file
import cv2 #For Image processing
import numpy as np #For converting Images
to Numerical array
import os #To handle directories
```

```
from PIL import Image #Pillow lib for handling images
face_cascade = cv2.CascadeClassifier('haarcascade_frontalface_default.xml')
recognizer = cv2.createLBPHFaceRecognizer()
Face_ID = -1
pev_person_name = ""
y_ID = []
x_train = []
Face_Images = os.path.join(os.getcwd(), "Face_Images") #Tell the program where we have saved the face images
print (Face_Images)
for root, dirs, files in os.walk(Face_Images): #go to the face image directory
for file in files: #check every directory in it
if file.endswith("jpeg") or file.endswith("jpg") or file.endswith("png"): #for image files ending with jpeg,jpg or png
path = os.path.join(root, file)
person_name = os.path.basename(root)
print(path, person_name)
if pev_person_name!=person_name: #Check if the name of person has changed
Face_ID=Face_ID+1 #If yes increment the ID count
```

```
pev_person_name = person_name
Gery_Image = Image.open(path).con-
vert("L") # convert the image to greysclae
using Pillow
Crop_Image = Gery_Image.resize( (550,550) ,
Image.ANTIALIAS) #Crop the Grey Image to
550*550 (Make sure your face is in the center
in all image)
Final_Image = np.array(Crop_Image, "uint8")
#print(Numpy_Image)
faces = face_cascade.detectMultiScale(
Final_Image, scaleFactor=1.5, minNeigh-
bors=5) #Detect The face in all sample image
print (Face_ID,faces)
for (x,y,w,h) in faces:
roi = Final_Image[y:y+h, x:x+w] #crop the
Region of Interest (ROI)
x_train.append(roi)
y_ID.append(Face_ID)
recognizer.train(x_train, np.array(y_ID))
#Create a Matrix of Training data
recognizer.save("face-trainner.yml") #Save
the matrix as YML file
```

❖ ❖ ❖

4. RASPBERRY PI DAC TUTORIAL: INTERFACING MCP4725 12-BIT DAC WITH RASPBERRY PI

Microcontrollers work just with computerized es-teems yet in genuine we need to manage Analog sign. That is the reason ADC is there to change over genuine Analog qualities into Digital structure with the goal that microcontrollers can process the sign. In any case, consider the possibility that we need Analog sign from advanced qualities, so here comes the DAC.

DAC can be utilized in numerous applications, for example, Motor control, Control Brightness of the LED Lights, Audio Amplifier, Video Encoders, Data Acquisition Systems and so forth.

We as of now interfaced MCP4725 DAC Module with Arduino and STM32. Today we will utilize the equivalent MCP4725 DAC IC to plan a DAC utilizing Raspberry Pi. It is expected that you have just introduced the most recent OS on your Raspberry PI and approach it by means of SSH. If not, pursue the

Getting started with Raspberry Pi instructional exercise before continuing. Here we are utilizing Rasbian Stretch introduced on Raspberry Pi 3.

Components Required

- Raspberry Pi 3 B+ (With Raspbian OS introduced)

- 16x2 LCD show

- MCP4725 DAC IC

- Interfacing Wires

- Breadboard

MCP4725 DAC Module (Digital to Analog Converter)

MCP4725 IC is a 12-Bit DAC Module which is utilized to produce yield simple voltages from (0 to 5V) and it is constrained by utilizing I2C correspondence. It additionally accompanies on board nonvolatile memory EEPROM.

This IC has 12-Bit goals. This implies we use (0 to 4096) as contribution to give the voltage yield regard to reference voltage. Greatest reference voltage is 5V.

Recipe to figure Output Voltage

O/P Voltage = (Reference Voltage / Resolution) x Digital Value

For Example on the off chance that we utilize 5V as reference voltage and we should expect that computerized worth is 2048. So to ascertain the DAC yield.

> **O/P Voltage = (5/ 4096) x 2048 = 2.5V**

Pinout of MCP4725

The following is the picture of MCP4725 with plainly demonstrating pin names.

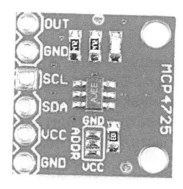

Pins of MCP4725	Use
OUT	Outputs Analog Voltage
GND	GND for Output
SCL	I2C Serial Clock line
SDA	I2C Serial Data line
VCC	Input Reference Volt-

	age 5V or 3.3V
GND	GND for input

This IC can be controlled utilizing the I2C corres-pondence which requires just two wires SCL and SDA. As a matter of course, the I2C address for MCP4725 is 0x60. Presently we think about I2C correspondence in Raspberry pi.

I2C pins in Raspberry Pi

So as to utilize MCP4725 with Raspberry Pi, the prin-cipal activity is knowing the Raspberry Pi I2C port sticks and arranging I2C port in the Raspberry pi.

The following is the Pin Diagram of Raspberry Pi 3 Model B+, and I2C pins GPIO2 (SDA) and GPIO3 (SCL) are utilized in this instructional exercise.

Designing I2C in Raspberry Pi

Of course, I2C is crippled in Raspberry Pi. So first it must be empowered. To empower the I2C in Rasp-berry Pi

1. Go to the terminal as well as type sudo raspi-config.

2. Presently the Raspberry Pi Software Configuration Tool shows up.

3. Select Interfacing alternatives and afterward em-power the I2C.

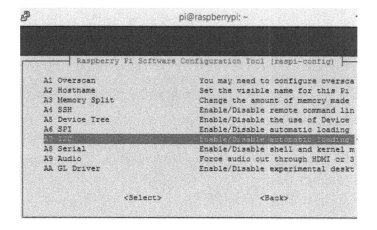

4. In the wake of empowering the I2C reboot the Pi.

Filtering I2C Address of MCP4725 utilizing Raspberry Pi

Presently so as to begin correspondence with the MCP4725 IC, the Raspberry Pi must realize its I2C address. To discover the location initially associate the SDA and SCL stick of MCP4725 to the SDA and SCL stick of Raspberry Pi. Likewise associate the +5V and GND pins.

Presently open the terminal and type underneath order to know the location of associated I2C gadget,

sudo i2cdetect –y 1 or **sudo i2cdetect –y 0**

Subsequent to finding the I2C address now its opportunity to introduce the essential libraries for utilizing MCP4725 with Raspberry Pi.

Installing MCP4725 Adafruit library into Raspberry Pi

So as to utilize MCP4725 DAC board with I2C transport of Raspberry Pi, an Adafruit MCP4725 library is utilized. To download and introduce the library pursue these means:

1. Ensure Raspberry Pi is associated with a functioning web.

2. Next open a terminal and show the accompanying lines balanced.

sudo apt-get install git build-essential python-dev

git clone https://github.com/adafruit/ Adafruit_Python_MCP4725.git

cd Adafruit_Python_MCP4725

sudo python setup.py install

3. After fruitful establishment now the Adafruit MCP4725 library can be imported in any python content by utilizing the line

Import Adafruit_MCP4725

Installing Adafruit LCD display library

A LCD is utilized in this venture to show the DAC and simple voltage esteems so to download and introduce the LCD library in Raspberry Pi pursue these means:

1. Open a terminal window and show the accompanying lines coordinated.

apt-get install git

git clone https://github.com/adafruit/ Adafruit_Python_CharLCD.git

cd Adafruit_Python_CharLCD

sudo python setup.py install

2. After establishment of LCD library now the Adafruit_python_CharLCD can be utilized from any python content by utilizing the accompanying line

import Adafruit_CharLCD as LCD

Presently the Raspberry Pi is prepared to code for DAC so how about we associate the circuit as appeared in the figure underneath.

Circuit Diagram and Connections

Circuit chart for utilizing DAC IC MCP4725 with Raspberry Pi is given underneath:

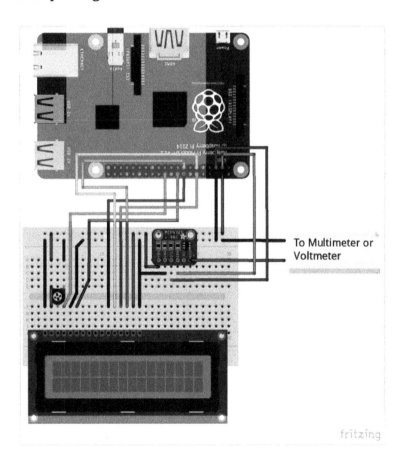

To Multimeter or Voltmeter

Circuit Connections between (16x2) LCD and Raspberry Pi

LCD	Raspberry Pi 3 B+
VSS	GND
VDD	+5V
V0	From potentiometer for contrast control
RS	GPIO25
RW	GND
E	GPIO24
D4	GPIO23
D5	GPIO17
D6	GPIO18
D7	GPIO22
A	+5V
K	GND

Circuit Connections between MCP4725 and Raspberry Pi

MCP4725	Raspberry Pi	Multimeter

	3 B+	
GND	GND	Negative Probe
VCC	+5V	-
SDA	GPIO2 (SDA)	-
SCL	GPIO3 (SCL)	-
OUT	-	Positive Probe

Complete arrangement will resemble this:

Programming Raspberry Pi for Digital to Analog Conversion

Complete Python code for Raspberry Pi is given toward the finish of this instructional exercise. Simply transfer it into raspberry pi utilizing any SSH customer like Putty or any FTP customer like FileZilla or you can straightforwardly compose program into raspberry pi by associating a screen to it. Become familiar with programming raspberry Pi here.

In this program a computerized estimation of 0-4096 is sent from Raspberry Pi to the MCP4725 by means of I2C transport to deliver a simple yield voltage of 0 to 5V which can be checked with the multimeter. Both the computerized and simple qualities are shown on the 16x2 LCD. In our program the computerized worth is sent with an augmentation of 150 utilizing for circle (0,150,300,450... 4050). We should see the program in detail.

First incorporate all the necessary libraries. Here LCD, MCP4725 and time library are utilized.

```
import Adafruit_CharLCD as LCD

import Adafruit_MCP4725

import time
```

Next characterize the LCD sticks alongside the no. of line and sections. We realize that 16X2 LCD has 2 lines and 16 sections. Become familiar with interfacing LCD with Raspberry Pi here.

```
lcd_rs    = 25
```

```
lcd_en     = 24

lcd_d4     = 23

lcd_d5     = 17

lcd_d6     = 18

lcd_d7     = 22

lcd_backlight = 4

# Define LCD column and row size for
16x2 LCD.

lcd_columns = 16

lcd_rows   = 2

lcd   =   LCD.Adafruit_CharLCD(lcd_rs,
lcd_en,    lcd_d4,    lcd_d5,    lcd_d6,
lcd_d7,lcd_columns, lcd_rows, lcd_back-
light)
```

Next show some invite message on LCD for five seconds.

lcd.message('Hello wolrd)

time.sleep(2.0)

lcd.message('\nDAC using Rpi')

time.sleep(5.0)

lcd.clear()

In the following line, a DAC example is made with the I2C address of the MCP4725 DAC IC. My board has a location of 0x60, change it as per your board.

dac = Adafruit_MCP4725.MCP4725(address=0x60)

Next a for circle is utilized inside while circle to change the advanced worth x that is sent to MCP4725 by means of I2C transport. The for circle run is (0,4095,150). The x esteems shift from 0 to 4050 with an addition of 150.

while True:

for x in range(0,4097,150):

The Digital worth is sent to MCP4725 utilizing the accompanying line

dac.set_voltage(x)

Contingent on the computerized worth the simple worth is determined utilizing the equation where 5 is reference voltage and x is advanced worth.

voltage = x/4096.0*5.0

At that point the Digital worth and Analog worth are shown on the LCD with a deferral of 2 seconds utilizing the accompanying lines

lcd.cursor_pos = (0,0)

lcd.message("DAC Value: " + str(x))

lcd.message("\nAnalogVolt: %.2f" % voltage)

time.sleep(2)

Here the Digital worth is appeared in the main line and simple incentive in second line of LCD show. A multimeter is likewise associated with the MCP4725 Output Pins to confirm the simple voltage.

Complete code is given beneath.

Code

```
import Adafruit_CharLCD as LCD
import Adafruit_MCP4725
import time
lcd_rs     = 25
lcd_en     = 24
lcd_d4     = 23
lcd_d5     = 17
lcd_d6     = 18
```

```
lcd_d7      = 22
lcd_backlight = 4
# Define LCD column and row size for 16x2
LCD.
lcd_columns = 16
lcd_rows   = 2
lcd = LCD.Adafruit_CharLCD(lcd_rs, lcd_en,
lcd_d4, lcd_d5, lcd_d6, lcd_d7,
                    lcd_columns, lcd_rows,
lcd_backlight)
lcd.message('Hello world)
time.sleep(2.0)
lcd.message('\nDAC using Rpi')
time.sleep(5.0)
lcd.clear()
dac = Adafruit_MCP4725.MCP4725(address-
=0x60)
while True:
  for x in range(0,4097,150):


    print(x)
   dac.set_voltage(x)
   lcd.cursor_pos = (0,0)
   lcd.message("DAC Value: " + str(x))
   voltage = x/4096.0*5.0
   lcd.message("\nAnalogVolt: %.2f" % volt-
```

```
age)
    time.sleep(2)
    lcd.clear()
```

❖ ❖ ❖

5. INTRODUCING OPENCV ON RASPBERRY PI UTILIZING CMAKE

Prior day's PC got input data from consoles and mouse, presently they have developed to have the option to process data from pictures and recordings. The capacity of a PC (machine) to extricate, dissect and comprehend data from a picture is called as Computer Vision. As of late the ability of Computer vision has gotten complex enough, not exclusively to perceive individuals/questions yet in addition to likewise examine their temperament or read even their feelings. All these were made conceivable with the assistance of profound learning/AI where a calculation prepared with numerous comparative pictures so it can search for data in another picture. Today the innovation has gotten solid enough to be utilized in Security, neighborliness and even in Financial Payment Portals.

The most regularly utilized library for Computer vision is OpenCV. It is an open source allowed to utilize cross-stage library from Intel, which means it could chip away at each working framework like windows, macintosh or Linux. We previously clarified introducing OpenCV on Windows and furthermore done some Image Manipulations utilizing Python OpenCV on Windows. Today we will figure out how to introduce the OpenCV4 library on Raspberry Pi 3 with the goal that we can utilize it for Computer vision applications. This will permits OpenCV to run on a compact gadget like Pi opening ways to numerous conceivable outcomes. So we should begin

Introducing OpenCV on Pi is an overwhelming procedure, predominantly on the grounds that it is very tedious and the odds of unearthing a mistake is high. So I have made this instructional exercise as basic and useful as conceivable dependent on the challenges that I had and ensuring you don't confront the equivalent. At the hour of composing this instructional exercise OpenCV has just discharged the 4.0.1 form three months back, yet I chose to adhere on to the past rendition that is 4.0.0 since the new form had some issue in getting aggregated.
Prerequisites

Before we make a plunge, I accept you have just introduced the most recent OS on your Raspberry PI and approach it by means of SSH. If not, pursue the Getting started with Raspberry Pi instructional exercise before continuing. Here I am utilizing Rasbian Stretch introduced on Raspberry Pi 3.

Pip Installing OpenCV on Raspberry PI

As we as a whole realize python has its very own bundle supervisor called pip which can be utilized to effectively include libraries for the python. What's more, yes there is additionally an approach to utilize PIP to introduce openCV inside minutes on Pi, yet unfortunately it didn't work for me and for some others too. Additionally introducing through pip doesn't enable us to oversee the OpenCV library, yet at the mean time on the off chance that you are searching for the speediest way, at that point you may try this out also.

Ensure pip is introduced on your pi and is moved up to most recent variant. At that point enter the accompanying directions on your terminal individually

sudo apt-get install libhdf5-dev libhdf5-serial-dev

sudo apt-get install libqtwebkit4 libqt4-test

sudo pip install opencv-contrib-python

This ought to introduce OpenCV on your Pi, in the

event that you are effective with this progression, at that point you can skirt the instructional exercise and look down to Step 13 to check if OpenCV is introduced appropriately with python. Else, take a full breath and start following the instructional exercise beneath.

Installing OpenCV 4 on Raspberry Pi using CMake

In this technique we will download the source bundle of OpenCV and accumulate it on our Raspberry Pi utilizing CMake. A few people will in general introduce OpenCV on virtual condition with the goal that they can utilize distinctive adaptation of python or OpenCV on a similar machine. In any case, I am not settling on that since I might want to keep this article short and furthermore I don't perceive any requirement for it at any point in the near future.

Stage 1: Before we start we should ensure the framework is refreshed to the present adaptation, to do this enter the accompanying direction

sudo apt-get update && sudo apt-get upgrade

This ought to download any most recent bundles if accessible and introduce it. The procedure will take 15-20 minutes so hang tight for it.

Stage 2: Next we need to refresh the able get bundle so we will have the option to download CMake in our following stage

```
sudo apt-get update
```

```
E: Package 'cmake' has no installation candidate
pi@raspberrypi:~ $ sudo apt-get install build-essential cmake unzip pkg-config
Reading package lists... Done
Building dependency tree
Reading state information... Done
Package cmake is not available, but is referred to by another package.
This may mean that the package is missing, has been obsoleted, or
is only available from another source

E: Package 'cmake' has no installation candidate
pi@raspberrypi:~ $ sudo apt-get update
Hit:1 http://archive.raspberrypi.org/debian stretch InRelease
Get:2 http://raspbian.raspberrypi.org/raspbian stretch InRelease [15.0 kB]
Get:3 http://raspbian.raspberrypi.org/raspbian stretch/main armhf Packages [11.7
 MB]
Get:4 http://raspbian.raspberrypi.org/raspbian stretch/contrib armhf Packages [5
6.9 kB]
Get:5 http://raspbian.raspberrypi.org/raspbian stretch/non-free armhf Packages [
95.5 kB]
Get:6 http://raspbian.raspberrypi.org/raspbian stretch/rpi armhf Packages [1,360
 B]
Fetched 11.8 MB in 32s (362 kB/s)
Reading package lists... Done
```

Stage 3: Once we have overhauled the adept get programming, we can download and introduce the CMake bundle utilizing the beneath order

sudo apt-get install build-essential cmake unzip pkg-config

Your screen would look like something like this beneath during the establishment of CMake

Stage 4: Then introduce the python 3 improvement headers utilizing the beneath order

sudo apt-get install python3-dev

Mine previously had it introduced so it shows something like this.

Stage 5: The following stage is download the OpenCV Zip document from GitHub. Utilize the accompanying direction to do likewise

wget -O opencv.zip https://github.com/ opencv/opencv/archive/4.0.0.zip

As should be obvious we are downloading the form 4.0.0

Stage 6: OpenCV has some pre-constructed bundles for python which will help us in creating stuff simpler called the OpenCV contrib. So how about we likewise download that by utilizing a comparative order that is demonstrated as follows.

wget -O opencv_con-trib.zip https://github.com/opencv/opencv_contrib/archive/4.0.0.zip

Now you ought to have downloaded two compress records named "opencv-4.0.0" and "opencv-contrib-4.0.0" on your home registry. You can look at it in the event of some unforeseen issue on the off chance that you need no doubt.

Stage 7: Lets unfasten the opencv-4.0.0 compress document utilizing the accompanying direction.

unzip opencv.zip

Stage 8: Similarly additionally remove the opencv_contrib-4.0.0 utilizing the order line

unzip opencv_contrib.zip

Stage 9: OpenCV requires numpy as an essential to work. So how about we introduce it utilizing the beneath order.

pip install numpy

Stage 10: Now, we would have two catalogs named "opencv-4.0.0" and "opencv_contrib-4.0.0" in our home index. The subsequent stage is assemble the Opencv library, to do that we have to make another index called "work" inside the opencv-4.0.0 catalog. Pursue the underneath directions to do likewise

cd~/opencv

mkdir build

cd build

Stage 11: Now, we need to run CMake for OpenCV. This is where we can arrange how OpenCV must be gathered. Ensure you are in the way "~/opencv-4.0.0/ form". At that point duplicate the beneath lines and past in the terminal window

```
cmake -D CMAKE_BUILD_TYPE=RELEASE \

  -D CMAKE_INSTALL_PREFIX=/usr/local \

  -D          OPENCV_EXTRA_MODULES_
PATH=~/opencv_contrib-4.0.0/modules \

  -D ENABLE_NEON=ON \

  -D ENABLE_VFPV3=ON \

  -D BUILD_TESTS=OFF \

  -D WITH_TBB=OFF \

  -D INSTALL_PYTHON_EXAMPLES=OFF \

  -D BUILD_EXAMPLES=OFF ..
```

It ought to get arranged with no blunders and you should see the content "Designing done" and "Creating done" in the as demonstrated as follows.

In case you get any mistake in this procedure, at that point ensure you have composed in the best possible way and you have two indexes named "opencv-4.0.0" and "opencv_contrib-4.0.0" in the home registry way.

Stage 12: This would be the most tedious advance. Again ensure you are in the way "~/opencv-4.0.0/ form" and utilize the accompanying direction to arrange OpenCV.

Make –j4

This would begin building OpenCV and you would have the option to see the improvement in rate. The procedure would take around 3-4 hours and in the event that it gets totally constructed you should see a screen like this above.

The direction "make – j4" utilizes all the four centers

to order OpenCV. At 99% rate a few people may think that its taking unreasonably long for the procedure to finish stand by calmly and it ought to get wrapped up.

For me it didn't work much subsequent to hanging tight for an hour thus I needed to prematurely end the procedure and construct it again utilizing "make – j1" and it worked. Utilizing make – j1 utilizes just single center of pi and it would require some investment than make j4 so it is prescribed to utilize make j4 and afterward utilizes make j1 since a wide portion of the aggregation would be finished by make j4.

Stage 13: If you have arrived at this progression at that point, that is it you have cruised through the procedure. The last advance is introduce libopecv utilizing the accompanying order.

sudo apt-get install libopencv-dev python-opencv

Stage 14: Finally you can check if the library was included effectively by running a basic python content. Type python and attempt "import cv2" like demonstrated as follows. You ought not get any mistake when you do this.

In the event that you get this screen, at that point you can continue in view of whatever OpenCV venture you have. In case you are simply beginning with OpenCV, at that point you can likewise investigate this Basic OpenCV instructional exercise. Additionally check our other Image handling instructional exercises.

Expectation this article had the option to help you in introducing OpenCV on Raspberry Pi, in the event that you have any issue post them in the remark area and I will attempt my best in getting it settled. You can likewise have a go at using our gatherings for progressively specialized inquiries.

6. RASPBERRY PI HEADLESS SETUP WITHOUT A MONITOR OR KEYBOARD

Any individual who is keen on finding out about PCs and gadgets will adore trying different things with a little and ground-breaking stage "Raspberry Pi". The main issue is that it doesn't have a screen and console mouse. This is really isn't an issue however, on the grounds that there is an approach to arrangement and work on the Pi without interfacing it to a screen and console. It is called headless on the grounds that it has no screen and console associated with it, so it is said to run headlessly.

Here, we will perceive how to set up a Raspberry Pi without a screen and console on another establishment of Raspbian.

Requirements

- Raspberry pi model B or above

- SD card peruser

- SD card (8 gb or above)

- 5v Adapter

- LAN link

- Workstation with working web association

We will pursue these means

1. Introducing Raspbian in SD card

2. Designing Network and Installing required virtual products in workstation

3. Booting of Raspberry pi

4. Associating Raspberry pi without Ethernet Installing Raspbian in SD card

Despite the fact that we have recently disclosed about how to introduce and design Raspberry pi in detail, here we again covering it quickly.

Stage 1:- There are numerous variants of OS for Raspberry Pi however Raspbian is progressively prominent. In this way, we will download OS picture of Raspbian Stretch from authentic webpage of raspberry pi.

Raspbian likewise has 3 three forms along these lines, download the ZIP record of Raspbian stretch with Desktop. As appeared in underneath picture

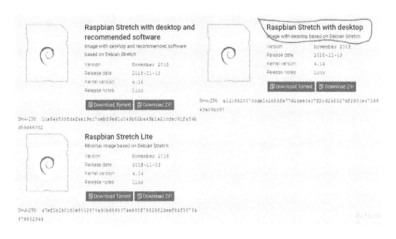

Stage 2:- After download is done, plug the SD card per-user in the USB port of PC with SD card in it to compose the downloaded arrangement in this SD card.

Stage 3:- Download the SD card formatter and OS flasher . Subsequent to downloading, introduce these virtual products individually. We will utilize these instruments to arrange the SD card appropriately and streak the Raspbian picture in it.

Stage 4:- Now, open SD card formatter and pick your SD card to arrange it as well as snap on Format.

Stage 5:- Open balena Etcher flasher and pick the area of Raspbian compress document that you have downloaded. Presently, pick the SD card and tap on streak.

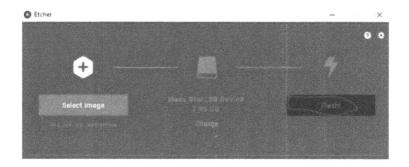

Stage 6:- After blazing is done, open SD card organizer. Make an unfilled record named as "ssh" with no expansion by right snap - > New - > Text report.

While renaming the document expel the .txt

This document is placed into SD card to empower the SSH (Secure Shell Login) in Raspberry Pi, on the grounds that Raspbian accompanies SSH debilitated as a matter of course.

Presently, we are prepared with the SD card. Fitting the SD card in the Raspberry pi card space.
Configuring network and Installing required softwares in Laptop

Stage 1:- In windows 10 , look for Network Settings - > Network and sharing focus. Here you will see dynamic wi-fi system to which your workstation associated.

Snap on your association name as appeared.

Stage 2:- Now, click on Properties. A Wi-Fi properties

exchange box will show up. Select the Internet Proto-
col Version 4 on the off chance that it isn't chosen.

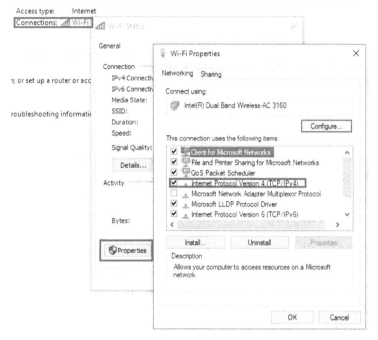

Stage 3:- Click on Sharing in a similar box and select
both the choices as appeared.

Snap on OK.

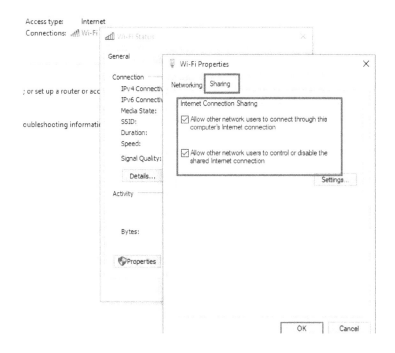

Stage 4:- Using above advances, an IP address is designated to our Raspberry Pi. Interface you Raspberry Pi with the PC utilizing Ethernet link and power on the pi.

Stage 5:- After interfacing your pi Ethernet link to workstation, you will see another Unidentified association underneath the dynamic systems.

View your basic network information and set up connections

View your active networks

LNMIIT-MME 2　　　　　　　Access type:　Internet
Public network　　　　　　　　Connections: ⚡ Wi-Fi (LNMIIT-MME)

Unidentified network　　　　Access type:　No network access
Public network　　　　　　　　Connections: ⚡ Ethernet

Change your networking settings

Stage 6:- Click on the Ethernet alternative of the system at that point click on Properties. Double tap on IpV4 .You will see entryway address of your pi. We will utilize this location go in Advance IP scanner.

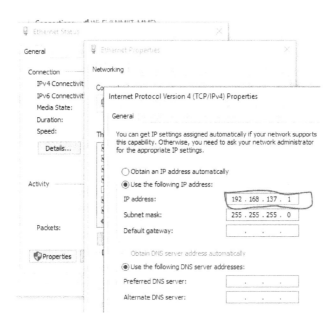

Stage 7:- Now, we need IP scanner programming and

SSH customer programming to converse with our raspberry pi. For this you can utilize Putty or MobaXterm . Download and introduce these programming projects. We will utilize MobaXterm as this product enable us to get to the work area of raspberry pi while putty permits terminal for the entrance of raspberry pi records.

Stage 8:- Copy that IP address that you have found in above advance and glue it in the inquiry bar of IP scanner and make the range as for my situation 192.168.137.1-254.

Booting of Raspberry Pi

Stage 1:- Now, this is your Raspberry pi's genuine IP address. Duplicate this IP address and open MobaXterm or putty. In MobaXterm click on Session - > SSH. Glue the location of Raspberry pi in Remote host space and snap on Ok .

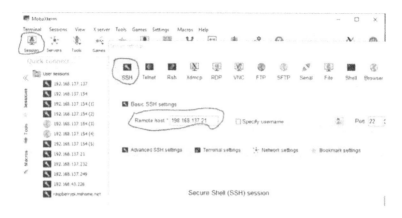

Stage 2:- You will be requested username and secret word of your pi. As a matter of course, Raspberry pi has username as "pi" and secret key is "raspberry". Enter these accreditations and hit enter.

Stage 3:- Now, this is your raspberry pi's terminal. You can get to anything inside your pi by utilizing various directions.

Stage 4:- For beginning the work area of your pi, type startlxde in the terminal and hit enter. The work area will show up as appeared. You can feel a similar work area experience likewise with the screen pi interface.

Stage 5:- To close the work area, click on Exit button in MobaXterm. In putty likewise, you can get the terminal same as past. It will resemble this.

```
pi@raspberrypi                                                    –    □    ×
login as: pi
pi@192.168.43.226's password:
Access denied
pi@192.168.43.226's password:
Linux raspberrypi 4.14.79-v7+ #1159 SMP Sun Nov 4 17:50:20 GMT 2018 armv7l

The programs included with the Debian GNU/Linux system are free software;
the exact distribution terms for each program are described in the
individual files in /usr/share/doc/*/copyright.

Debian GNU/Linux comes with ABSOLUTELY NO WARRANTY, to the extent
permitted by applicable law.
Last login: Tue Dec 11 12:39:07 2018 from 192.168.43.183

SSH is enabled and the default password for the 'pi' user has not been changed.
This is a security risk - please login as the 'pi' user and type 'passwd' to set
 a new password.

pi@raspberrypi:~ $ []
```

To shutdown the Raspberry pi type this direction sudo shutdown now and hit enter.

Thus, this is the way you can get to your Pi without having additional screen and console. However, once in a while we can't get the IP address of the pi utilizing Ethernet association. To defeat this issue, we can interface the Raspberry Pi with the workstation without Ethernet association.

Presently in following stages we will perceive how to associate your Pi without Ethernet.
Connecting Raspberry Pi without Ethernet

For this strategy, your Rpi and PC ought to be associated with same Wi-Fi arrange. We have to spare the Wi-Fi accreditations by making another record in pi's SD card. In this way, expel the SD card from the Rpi and addition it in card peruser and plug that peruser in PC.

Stage 1:- Go to Boot registry of the card. Make a book document with the name wpa_supplicant.conf and open this record utilizing scratch pad. Glue the underneath code in this record Replace the YOUR-SSID and PASSWORD with your Wi-FI system's accreditations and spare it.

ctrl_interface=DIR=/var/run/wpa_supplicant GROUP=netdev

update_config=1

network={

ssid="YOUR-SSID"

psk="YOUR-PASSWORD"

scan_ssid=1

}

Stage 2:- Now, plug the sd card in your Pi and power it on. I am utilizing my telephone's hotspot to associate the PC and Pi. In case you are utilizing Router, at that point Open your remote switch's setup page. From that point, you can discover switch's DHCP rent table and note the Pi's IP address.

Stage 3:- To discover the IP address while utilizing telephone's hotspot, you have to introduce Hotspot supervisor application in your cell phone from this connection.

Stage 4:- Open the Hotspot supervisor application and make your hotspot certifications.

Stage 5:- Tap on Clients and revive it. From the run-down given you can see the IP address of your PI.

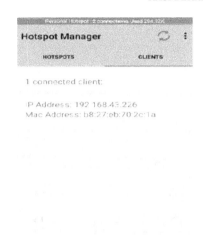

Utilize this IP address in putty or MobaXterm to associate your Raspberry Pi headlessly as well as you are prepared with to get to anything in your Raspberry Pi.

7. BEGINNING WITH NODE.JS AS WELL AS RASPBERRY PI: CONTROLLING A LED WITH NODE.JS WEBSERVER

In past Raspberry Pi Tutorials, we have utilized a large range of programming dialects and virtual products to control Raspberry Pi including Python, implanted C, Flask and so forth. To grow the skyline of incredible Raspberry Pi board, today we will utilize a mainstream JavaScript based condition (Node.js) to control Raspberry Pi GPIOs locally just as all around by setting it up as webserver. At first, Node.js was created for Google Chrome yet later it was publicly released by Google.

In this instructional exercise, we will control a LED, associated with Raspberry Pi, utilizing two strategies

- First we will essentially compose a JavaScript code utilizing Node.js to Blink the LED

- In second technique, we will make a HTML page with two catches to kill on and the LED.

This HTML website page will be facilitated on raspberry pi and can be opened on any internet browser. So here Raspberry Pi will go about as webserver

Materials Required

- Raspberry pi board with Raspbian introduced in it

- Driven

In this instructional exercise I am utilizing External Monitor utilizing HDMI link to interface with Raspberry Pi. On the off chance that you don't have screen, you can utilize SSH customer (Putty) or VNC server to interface with Raspberry pi utilizing Laptop or PC. In the event that you discover any trouble, at that point pursue our Getting gazed with Raspberry Pi Guide. Installing Node.js on Raspberry Pi

We will introduce Node.js in our board utilizing the accompanying directions.

Stage 1:- First check for the arm variant of your raspberry pi board utilizing this order.

```
uname -m
```

For my situation, form is 7.

Stage 2:- Download the installer by duplicating this connection in the terminal. Remember to change the form in the connection given underneath.

wget   https://nodejs.org/dist/v4.6.1/ node-v4.6.1-linux-armv[version]l.tar.gz

Stage 3:- Extract the records utilizing beneath order

tar   -xvf   node-v4.6.1-linux-armv[version]l.tar.gz

Stage 4:- Finally, execute these directions to add the significant records to neighborhood indexes too.

cd node-v4.3.1-linux-armv[version]l

sudo cp -R * /usr/local/

Node.js is introduced now in your Raspberry Pi. Check the variant of hub for affirmation utilizing this direction.

node –version

Prior to going to make a Node.js server, first we will

perceive how to compose a content to flicker a LED utilizing node.js (npm onoff bundle).
Blinking an LED using Node.js

To control the GPIO on the Raspberry Pi utilizing Node.js, we will utilize onoff module.

We will utilize npm bundle chief to introduce onoff module utilizing underneath order

npm install onoff

Presently, we will compose a content for squinting of drove. Open nano editorial manager and give the name to document utilizing the order

nano blink_led.js

In case you are an apprentice in Node.js and it's bundles, you can the documentation of npm for better comprehension of the content.
Node.js LED Blink script and Explanation

To start with, announce the factors for drove, postponement and GPIO. I am utilizing Raspberry Pi GPIO 4 to interface the LED.

var Gpio = require('onoff').Gpio;

```
var LED = new Gpio(4, 'out');

var blinkInterval = setInterval(blinkLED,
500);
```

Presently, we will make a capacity to begin the squint.

```
function blinkLED() {

  if (LED.readSync() === 0) {

    LED.writeSync(1); //set output to 1 i.e
turn led on

  } else {

    LED.writeSync(0); //set output to 0 i.e.
turn led off

  }

}
```

Correspondingly, make a capacity to stop the flickering

```
function endBlink() {

  clearInterval(blinkInterval);

  LED.writeSync(0);

  LED.unexport(); // Unexport GPIO to free
resources

}

setTimeout(endBlink, 10000);
```

Complete Node.js code for Blinking LED is given toward the finish of this instructional exercise. So reorder the code in the document led_blink.js, which we have made already utilizing nano order, spare the record utilizing Ctrl+x, at that point press Y and hit enter.

To run the content, open the terminal and type the underneath order:

```
node blink_led.js
```

You will see that LED will flicker for 10 seconds and after that it quit squinting. Check the total working in the Video given in end of this instructional exercise.

Circuit Diagram for Blinking an LED using Node.js

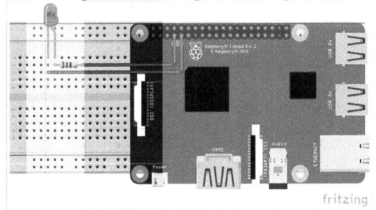

Raspberry Pi Webserver using Node.js

Presently, go to the fascinating part, here we are going to make our own web server from which we can control GPIO of Raspberry pi utilizing a website page.

For this, first we have to make a HTML page and compose a content to perform back-end task for example to control the RPi GPIO.

Stage 1:- Make a registry to store every one of the documents at one spot.

```
mkdir nodejs_server
```

Stage 2:- Inside the nodejs_server organizer make one more envelope for sparing the HTML record.

```
cd nodejs_server

mkdir views
```

Stage 3:- If you need to add pictures to your html page, at that point you should make another envelope named open inside the primary registry for example in nodejs_server organizer. In the open envelope, make picture organizer and store every one of the pictures in this organizer.

Stage 4:- Now, we will make HTML page. For this, go to sees catalog and open nano content manager with filename index.ejs

There is nothing extravagant in the content. It is only a HTML document to make On and Off catch.

Duplicate glue the underneath HTML code in nano word processor and spare it.

```html
<meta name="viewport" content=
"width=500, initial-scale=1">

<div class="BorderMargin">

<image src = '/images/anbazhagank.jpg'
alt="LED"
style="width:500px;height:250px;"
align="left">

<h1>Welcome to Nodejs Server</h1>

<form action="/led/on" method="post">

<button type="submit"
class="button">LED On </button>

<button type="submit" form-
method="post" formaction="/led/off"
class="button button3">LED Off</but-
ton>

</form>

<a>Led Status: <%=status %></a>
```

```
</div>
```

Stage 5:- Now, we need to compose JavaScript code. We are utilizing hub express system to react to http demands performed by the client.

You can pursue the connection to get familiar with Node Express.

Open terminal and open nano content tool with index.js filename in nodejs_server envelope, at that point reorder the underneath java content code and this document.

```
var express = require('express');

var app = express();

var path = require('path');

var gpio = require('rpi-gpio');

gpio.setup(7, gpio.DIR_OUT);

app.set('view engine', 'ejs');

app.use(express.static(path.join(__dirname, 'public')));
```

```
console.log(path.join(__dirname,    'pub-
lic'));

app.get('/', function(req, res){

 res.render('index',{status:"Press    But-
ton"});

});

app.post('/led/on', function(req, res){

gpio.write(7, true, function(err) {

    if (err) throw err;

    console.log('Written True to pin');

console.log(path.join(__dirname,    'pub-
lic'));

return res.render('index', {status: "Led is
On"});

  });

});
```

```
app.post('/led/off', function(req, res){

gpio.write(7, false, function(err) {

    if (err) throw err;

    console.log('Written False to pin');

console.log(path.join(__dirname,    'pub-
lic'));

return res.render('index',{status: "Led is
Off"});

  });

});

app.listen(3000, function () {

 console.log('Server    Started    on    Port:
3000!')

})
```

Stage 6:- Inside the nodejs_server catalog, we need to execute following direction to introduce libraries of node.js

npm install

Stage 7:- Now, your server is prepared to work. To begin the neighborhood server, run the accompanying order inside the nodejs_server catalog

node index.js

you will see a message in the terminal that your server is begun at the characterized port.

Stage 8:- Now open your program and open Raspberry Pi URL with port number for example raspberrypi:3000

Ensure that your raspberry pi as well as PC in which you are opening the program are associated with a similar system.

You will see the accompanying page in the program.

135

Welcome to Nodejs Server

LED On | LED Off

Led Status: Led is Off

Presently, press LED On catch to turn on the LED and LED Off catch to kill the LED.

Code

Code for blinking LED using Node.js

```
var Gpio = require('onoff').Gpio;
var LED = new Gpio(4, 'out');
var blinkInterval = setInterval(blinkLED, 500);
function blinkLED() {
 if (LED.readSync() === 0) {
   LED.writeSync(1); //set output to 1 i.e turn led on
 } else {
   LED.writeSync(0); //set output to 0 i.e. turn led off
 }
}
function endBlink() {
 clearInterval(blinkInterval);
```

```
LED.writeSync(0);
  LED.unexport(); // Unexport GPIO to free
resources
}
setTimeout(endBlink, 10000);
```

Code for blinking LED using Node.js web-server

```
var express = require('express');
var app = express();
var path = require('path');
var gpio = require('rpi-gpio');
gpio.setup(7, gpio.DIR_OUT);
app.set('view engine', 'ejs');
app.use(express.static(path.join(__dirname,
'public')));
console.log(path.join(__dirname, 'public'));
app.get('/', function(req, res){
 res.render('index',{status:"Press Button"});
});
app.post('/led/on', function(req, res){
gpio.write(7, true, function(err) {
    if (err) throw err;
    console.log('Written True to pin');
console.log(path.join(__dirname, 'public'));
return  res.render('index',  {status:  "Led  is
On"});
```

```
  });
});
app.post('/led/off', function(req, res){
gpio.write(7, false, function(err) {
    if (err) throw err;
    console.log('Written False to pin');
console.log(path.join(__dirname, 'public'));
return    res.render('index',{status:    "Led    is
Off"});
  });
});
app.listen(3000, function () {
  console.log('Server Started on Port: 3000!')
})
```

◆ ◆ ◆

8. MANUFACTURE YOUR OWN GOOGLE HOME UTILIZING A RASPBERRY PI

Have you at any point considered a speaker which can be constrained by your voice!!! Truly, Amazon Echo is the one of the most prominent voice controlled Speaker, however in rivalry with it Google Home is additionally getting well known. Voice associates getting increasingly mainstream as we are going towards a period of AI based frameworks. You have caught wind of Google Assistant, Apple Siri and Amazon Alexa. These all are Voice based AI frameworks, what makes these not quite the same as one another is their biological systems, and this is the place Google Assistant champion the most. Google, Apple and Amazon, every one of these organizations previously propelled their savvy speakers. Google savvy speakers are additionally accessible in the market. We previously secured Raspberry Pi based Amazon Echo, this time we will transform Raspberry Pi into a Google Home Speaker.

Google gives the API to utilizing its voice administration, which is open source and accessible on Github. Utilizing Google voice administration, we can play music, get data about climate, book tickets and some more. You should simply Ask. In this instructional exercise, how about we perceive how to fabricate a voice controlled brilliant speaker utilizing Google colleague and Raspberry Pi.

Hardware Requirements

- Raspberry Pi 3 [Recommended] or Raspberry Pi 2 Model B [Supported] as well as Secure Digital card(8Giga Byte or more)

- Outside Speaker with 3.5mm AUX link

- Any Webcam or Universal Serial Bus 2.0 Microphone

We likewise accept that your Raspberry pi is as of now set up with a Raspbian OS as well as is associated with the web. With these set up we should continue with the instructional exercise. In the event that you are new to Raspberry Pi, at that point experience Getting started with Raspberry pi first.

Note: Webcam has inbuilt amplifier in this way, we will utilize this instead of USB 2.0 receiver.

You additionally need a console, mouse and a screen to associate the raspberry pi utilizing HDMI link.

Checking Webcam Mic with Raspberry Pi:

1. Open Raspberry Pi terminal as well as type arecord -l order. This will show the equipment gadgets which are associated with Raspberry Pi as demonstrated as follows:

File Edit Tabs Help

```
   st-nowait        do not wait for ring buffer - eats whole CPU
   x-file-time=#    start another output file when the old file has recorded
                    for this many seconds
 --process-id-file  write the process ID here
 --use-strftime     apply the strftime facility to the output file name
 --dump-hw-params   dump hw_params of the device
 --fatal-errors     treat all errors as fatal
Recognized sample formats are: S8 U8 S16_LE S16_BE U16_LE U16_BE S24_LE S24_BE U
24_LE U24_BE S32_LE S32_BE U32_LE U32_BE FLOAT_LE FLOAT_BE FLOAT64_LE FLOAT64_BE
 IEC958_SUBFRAME_LE IEC958_SUBFRAME_BE MU_LAW A_LAW IMA_ADPCM MPEG GSM SPECIAL S
24_3LE S24_3BE U24_3LE U24_3BE S20_3LE S20_3BE U20_3LE U20_3BE S18_3LE S18_3BE U
18_3LE U18_3BE G723_24 G723_24_1B G723_40 G723_40_1B DSD_U8 DSD_U16_LE DSD_U32_L
E DSD_U16_BE DSD_U32_BE
Some of these may not be available on selected hardware
The available format shortcuts are:
-f cd (16 bit little endian, 44100, stereo)

pi@raspberrypi

pi@raspberrypi
```

Card 1 is your webcam's mic that we are gonna to utilize. On the off chance that it isn't shown, your webcam might be flawed.

2. Presently, check if mic is working by running the record sound direction as:

arecord /home/pi/Desktop/test.wav -D sysdefault:CARD=1

3. To play the recorded sound sort this direction:

omxplayer -p -o local /home/pi/Desktop/test.wav

On the off chance that you have associated Raspberry

Pi with screen utilizing HDMI link, at that point as a matter of course sound yield is through your screen's speaker (if there is inbuilt speaker in it). In this way, to transform it to 3.5mm you need to type the accompanying order:

sudo raspi-config and go to Advance option.

Select Audio from the rundown - > select Force 3.5mm - > select Ok and Restart you Raspberry Pi.

Presently, you ought to hear the sound from 3.5mm jack.

NOTE: If you need to increment or diminishing the information voice tumult for mouthpiece the sort alsamixer in the terminal. Select sound card from the terminal by squeezing F6.

Press F4 to change the Mic dB pick up and set it as you need.

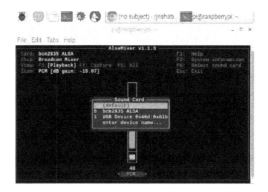

On the off chance that you have USB 2.0 receiver, at that point steps pursued are same to check the amplifier. Here we have utilized Webcam for USB microcphone.

Setting up the Google API for Raspberry Pi Google Assistant

1. To begin with, we need to enlist and set up a venture on the Google Console Actions dashboard .

2. In the wake of signing in to your Google account, you will see following window.

Snap on Add/Import Project.

3. On next screen, you need to enter the Project Name and tap on Create Project.

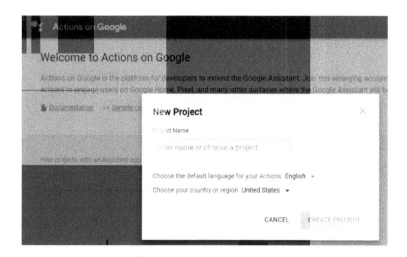

4. Presently, go to the Google designers reassure in the

new tab and quest for Google Assistant API. Before you feel free to press the Enable catch make sure that you have your venture chosen. At that point click on Enable.

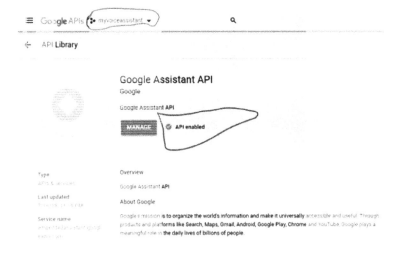

5. Presently, open the past tab of Google comfort and look down to the base of the screen.

You will discover an alternative Device Registration, click on it.

6. On the following screen, Click on Register Model. After this, you have to set a Product Name, Manufacturer name and set a Device Type. These names can be anything as you need.

Record the Device Model Id, as we will require this later all the while.

Presently, click on Register Model.

7. Next screen will be for Download Credentials. To get this certifications document click the Download OAuth 2.0 qualifications. This document is significant in this way, keep it some place safe.

Presently, click on Next.

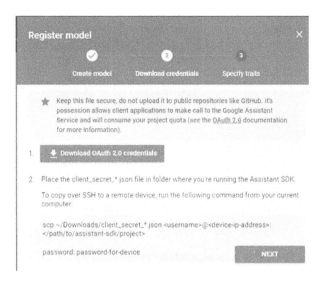

8. You can choose any qualities that you need, however for our situation we needn't bother with any of these so we just tapped the Skip button as demonstrated as follows.

9. Once everything is done, you will have following screen.

10. Presently, go to Activity Controls page. Here you need to initiate the accompanying movement controls to guarantee that the Google Assistant API work fine.

Web as well as App Activity, Location History, Device Information, Voice as well as Audio Activity

11. Once more, go to Google designers support . Snap on Credentials on the left half of dashboard. Snap on OAuth assent screen.

12. Fill your Gmail id and any name to the Product name and Save it.

Presently, we have finished with the Google API arrangement.

Setting up Google Assistant for Raspberry Pi Google Home

It would be ideal if you note from this part onwards you will be required to finish the instructional exercise on the Raspbian work area straightforwardly and not over SSH, this is since you should utilize the inherent internet browser.

1. In the first place, update the Raspberry Pi's bundle list by utilizing the accompanying order

sudo apt-get update

2. Presently, we will make a document where we can store the certifications we downloaded before. For this, run the accompanying two directions

mkdir ~/googleassistant

nano ~/googleassistant/credentials.json

3. In this document, you need to duplicate the substance of the qualifications record that we downloaded. Open the .json record in your preferred word processor and press ctrl + A then ctrl + C to duplicate the substance.

In case of replicating the substance, spare the record by squeezing Ctrl + X then Y and afterward at long last press Enter .

4. Subsequent to sparing the accreditations document, we will begin introducing a portion of the conditions required to run the Google partner.

Run the accompanying order to introduce Python3 and the Python 3 Virtual Environment to our RPi.

sudo apt-get install python3-dev python3-venv

5. Presently empower python3 as our virtual condi-

tion utilizing following direction

```
python3 -m venv env
```

6. Introduce the most recent variants of pip and the setuptools. Run following order to get the update

```
env/bin/python -m pip install --upgrade pip setuptools --upgrade
```

7. To get into the python condition, we need to run this direction

```
source env/bin/activate
```

8. Presently we will introduce the Google Assistant Library, show the accompanying directions coordinated to get the refreshed library

```
python -m pip install --upgrade google-assistant-library
```

```
python -m pip install --upgrade google-assistant-sdk[samples]
```

Presently, we have wrapped up all the necessary conditions and libraries.

Authorizing Raspberry Pi for the Google Assistant

1. We will initially introduce the Google approval device to our Raspberry pi by executing the accompanying direction

python -m pip install --upgrade google-auth-oauthlib[tool]

2. Presently, we have to run the Google Authentication library. Execute this direction to run the library.

**google-oauthlib-tool --client-secrets ~/ googleassistant/credentials.json **

**--scope   https://www.googleapis.com/ auth/assistant-sdk-prototype **

**--scope   https://www.googleapis.com/ auth/gcm **

--save –headless

This direction will create a URL, duplicate this URL and glue it in your internet browser.

3. In the program, login to your Google account, on the off chance that you have various records just select the one you set up your API key with.

After login, you will view a long confirmation code. Duplicate this code and glue it into your terminal window and press enter. On the off chance that the validation is checked you should view the accompanying line show up on order line as appeared in above picture:

> credentials saved: /home/pi/.config/goo-gle-oauthlib-tool/credentials.json

4. Our validation qualifications are confirmed currently, yet Google still need to check through a pop show. However, our spring up is obstructed by the CORS(Cross-beginning asset sharing) along these lines, first debilitate this thing utilizing underneath order.

To utilize this direction ensure your chromium program is shut and now open new terminal window and type the order. This direction will dispatch the chromium program with the CORS security impaired, don't peruse the web with this crippled.

> **chromium-browser --disable-web-security --user-data-dir "/home/pi/**

After the opening of program, go to the past terminal window where you have arrangement the Google right hand test.

5. Presently run the accompanying direction to first time dispatch of Google right hand. In this direction

supplant <projectid> with the id of your venture.

On the off chance that you overlooked the Project ID, go to Actions Console on Google, click the venture you made, at that point click the rigging symbol in the upper left-hand corner at that point Project Settings.

Additionally, supplant <deviceid> with the gadget ID that you acquired before in the instructional exercise.

---

googlesamples-assistant-pushtotalk -- project-id <projectid> --device-model-id <deviceid> --display

---

This order will dispatch another tab in the Chromium program.

6. Presently press Enter in the terminal window to trigger it and pose any inquiry.

At the point when you posed the main inquiry, beneath screen may show up in the program. Snap on Continue - > I comprehend - > Allow.

On the off chance that this Continue screen not shows up, no issue.

7. Presently, we can utilize push to talk Google Assistant example and get a yield reaction.

At the point when you press the Enter in the terminal and talk an activity you ought to hear a verbal reaction and another tab will likewise opened showing the activity you just called.

You can debilitate the opening of tab by expelling the – show contention from the order. We required this to get the approval screen.
Using Google Assistant on Raspberry Pi

We have approved our Raspberry Pi. At whatever point you need to dispatch Google colleague, simply get in the earth and pursue the beneath steps.

1. Run the accompanying direction on get in nature

source env/bin/activate

You will see (env) show up at the front of each line.

2. To fire up the push to talk test, run the accompanying direction

googlesamples-assistant-pushtotalk

This time we needn't bother with item id and gadget id.

3. Notwithstanding the push to talk include, you can likewise trigger the Google aide by saying Ok Google. For this you need to enter an invalid gadget id for it to work. Off base gadget id can be in any way similar to aaaa, abcd.

Presently, run the accompanying direction.

googlesamples-assistant-hotword --device-model-id <deviceid>

```
File Edit Tabs Help
pi@raspberrypi:~ $ source env/bin/activate
(env) pi@raspberrypi:~ $ googlesamples-assistant-hotword --device-model-id abcd
device_model_id: abcd
device_id: AF3D39D01A030548B5BE0077A233E763

    This device is not registered. This means you will not be able to use
    Device Actions or see your device in Assistant Settings. In order to
    register this device follow instructions at:

    https://developers.google.com/assistant/sdk/guides/library/python/embed/regi
ster-device

ON_MUTED_CHANGED:
  {"is_muted": false}
ON_START_FINISHED

ON_CONVERSATION_TURN_STARTED
ON_END_OF_UTTERANCE
ON_RECOGNIZING_SPEECH_FINISHED:
  {"text": "what is the temperature in Jaipur"}
ON_RENDER_RESPONSE:
  {"text": "It's a scorcher today!", "type": 0}
ON_RENDER_RESPONSE:
{
  "text": "In Jaipur right now, it's 94.\n---\n( More on weather.com )",
  "type": 0
}
```

Presently, you can ask anything with the own one of a kind Google right hand simply state Ok Google.

So this is the means by which we can introduce Google Assistant on Raspberry Pi and can transform it into a Google Home by associating a Speaker and receiver to it.

9. INTERFACING 3.5 INCH TOUCH SCREEN TFT LCD WITH RASPBERRY PI

Raspberry Pi is a Palm Size PC that comes in exceptionally helpful when prototyping stuff that requires high computational power. It is as a rule broadly utilized for IOT equipment improvement and mechanical technology application and considerably more memory hunger applications. In the greater part of the ventures including the Pi it would be amazingly valuable if the Pi had a showcase through which we can screen the vitals of our task.

The pi itself has a HDMI yield which can be straightforwardly associated with a Monitor, however in ventures where space is an oblige we need littler presentations. So in this instructional exercise we will figure out how we can interface the well known 3.5 inch Touch Screen TFT LCD screen from waveshare with

Raspberry pi. Toward the finish of this instructional exercise you will have a completely useful LCD show with contact screen over your Pi fit to be utilized for your future activities.

The specialized particular of the 3.5" TFT LCD screen is demonstrated as follows.

LCD Type	TFT
Size	3.5
Resolution	320*480 Pixels
Interface	SPI
Display Controller	XPT2046
Touch Type	Resistive
Backlight	LED
Aspect Ratio	8:5
Colours	65536
Supports	Camera, Mouse and Keyboard

Materials Required
  • Raspberry Pi
  • Internet connection
  • 3.5" TFT LCD
Pre-Requisites

It is accepted that your Raspberry Pi is as of now flashed with a working framework and can associate with the web. If not, pursue the Getting started with Raspberry Pi instructional exercise before continuing.

It is likewise accepted that you approach the terminal window of your raspberry pi. In this instructional exercise we will utilize Putty in SSH mode to associate with the Raspberry Pi. You can utilize any strategy however you ought to by one way or another have the option to approach your Pi's terminal window.

Connecting your Raspberry Pi with TFT LCD screen

Associating your 3.5" TFT LCD screen with Raspberry pi is a cake walk. The LCD has a piece of female header pins which will fit cozy into the male header pins. You simply need to adjust the pins and press the LCD over the Pi to make the association. When fixed appropriately you Pi and LCD will look something like this underneath. Note that I have utilized a packaging for my Pi so overlook the white box.

For individuals who are interested to comprehend what these pins are! It is utilized to build up a SPI correspondence between the Raspberry Pi and LCD as well as furthermore to control the LCD from the 5V and 3.3V stick of the raspberry Pi. Aside from that it additionally has a few pins devoted for the touch screen to work. Absolutely there are 26 sticks, the image and portrayal of the pins are demonstrated as follows

Pin No:	Symbol	Description
1, 17	3.3V	3.3V power input
2,4	5V	5V power input
3,5,7,8,10,12,13,15,16	NC	No connection – used for support
6,9,14,20,25	GND	Ground

11	TP_IRQ	Active low interrupt pin for touch screen
18	LCD_RS	Register select pin of Display controller
19	LCD_SI	SPI data input for the LCD display
21	TP_SO	SPI data output from the LCD display
22	RST	Reset
23	LCD_SCK	Clock sync pin of SPI communication
24	LCD_CS	Chip select pin of SPI LCD
26	TP_CS	Chip select pin of SPI Touch screen

Preparing your Raspberry Pi for 3.5" LCD Display Screen

Presently, in case of interfacing the LCD to PI, control the PI and you will see a clear white screen on the LCD. This is on the grounds that there are no drivers introduced on our PI to utilize the associated LCD. So let us open the terminal window of Pi as well as start making the vital changes. Once more, I am utilizing putty to interface with my Pi you can utilize your helpful technique.

Stage 1: Get into the design window utilizing the accompanying order. To get the beneath window

sudo raspi-config

Stage 2: Navigate to Boot Options - > Desktop/CLI and select choice B4 Desktop Autologin Desktop GUI, naturally signed in as 'pi' client as featured in beneath

picture. This will make the PI to login naturally from next boot without the client entering the secret key.

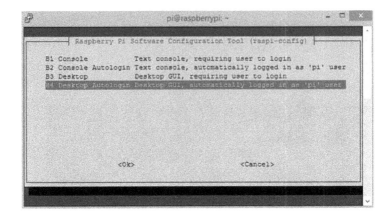

Stage 3: Now again explore to interfacing choices and empower SPI as show in the picture beneath. We need to empower the SPI interface on the grounds that as we examined the LCD and PI imparts through SPI convention

Stage 4: Click on this waveshare driver connect to download the driver as a ZIP document. At that point move the ZIP document to you PI OS. I utilized Filezilla to do this, yet you can likewise utilize a pen drive and straightforward duplicate glue work. Mine was put in the way/home/pi.

Stage 5: After the compress document is put in position proceed with your terminal window. To introduce the driver utilize the accompanying order.

tar xvf LCD-show-*.tar.gz

Note: Make sure your PI is associated with web during this progression

Stage 6: Finally in the wake of introducing the driver we can empower the showcase by utilizing the underneath direction

cd LCD-show/

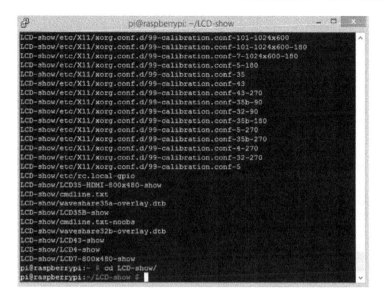

Stage 7: Now utilize the beneath direction to restart your Pi. This will naturally end the terminal window. At the point when the PI restarts you should see the LCD show additionally indicating the boot data lastly the work area will show up as demonstrated as follows.

sudo reboot

check how the LCD is associated and how it reacts to contact. I am essentially happy with its default exactness so I won't do any alignment. Be that as it may, on the off chance that you are intrigued you can see the authority wiki page from waveshare where they talk about how to adjust and empower camera see on the LCD screen.

Expectation you comprehended the instructional exercise and were fruitful in interfacing your LCD with PI and made it work.

10. SET UP A MINECRAFT SERVER ON YOUR RASPBERRY PI

Minecraft is the most prevalent game on the planet and individuals are getting added substance for this intriguing game. You can arrangement your own Minecraft server and can make your own universes in the game. For this, you don't have to burn through cash on a committed PC, it very well may be effectively finished with a little, charge card measured Linux PC Raspberry Pi. On the off chance that you need to play it on little LAN coordinate with your loved ones then Raspberry is the ideal decision for you. Illustrations of this game isn't great yet at the same time it looks so entrancing to play this game on connect with others.

Inside 60 minutes, you can begin playing Minecraft on your devoted Raspberry Pi controlled Minecraft server. Notwithstanding, Raspberry Pi isn't ground-breaking enough to deal with high complex robotized homesteads and in excess of 5 players yet at the same time is it one the best ease alternative to play this fascinating game on organize.

Thus, in this instructional exercise we will find out about overseeing Minecraft servers utilizing Raspberry Pi.

Requirements

1. Raspberry pi 2 or above with Raspbian introduced in it

2. LAN link

3. Power connector

In this instructional exercise I am utilizing External Monitor utilizing HDMI link to interface with Raspberry Pi. In case you don't have screen, you can utilize SSH customer (Putty) or VNC server to interface with Raspberry pi utilizing Laptop or PC. In case you discover any trouble, at that point pursue our Getting gazed with Raspberry Pi Guide.

To interface with this Minecraft server you need another Raspberry Pi to join the game. Here the total procedure to arrangement minecraft on Rasbperry pi is clarified in the beneath steps:
1. Update the Raspberry Pi

First refresh and redesign your raspberry pi framework utilizing this order:

sudo apt-get update && sudo apt-get -y upgrade

2. Setup Your Environment

Minecraft chips away at Java thus, check whether Java and java compiler is introduced in your Raspberry Pi utilizing the accompanying directions:

java -version

javac –version

```
java -version

java version "1.8.0_181"
Java(TM) SE Runtime Environment (build 1.8.0_181-b13)
Java HotSpot(TM) Client VM (build 25.181-b13, mixed mode)

javac -version

javac 1.8.0_181
```

Your form can be extraordinary. In the event that adaptations are not appearing, at that point you need to introduce java SDK.

3. Install Minecraft

We will introduce Spigot Minecraft Server, It is a most streamline module for little Minecraft servers. Following are steps to do that:

Stage 1: Create the Minecraft envelope

```
cd /home/pi

  mkdir minecraft

  cd minecraft
```

Stage 2: Download the buildtools

```
sudo  wget  https://hub.spigotmc.org/
jenkins/job/BuildTools/lastSuccessful-
Build/artifact/target/BuildTools.jar
```

Stage 3: Build the server bundle that you have down-loaded utilizing beneath order:

```
sudo java -jar BuildTools.jar
```

Working of the records requires some investment. It will take around one hour to two hours relying upon your web speed. Along these lines, this would be a decent time to get yourself a beverage or tidbits.

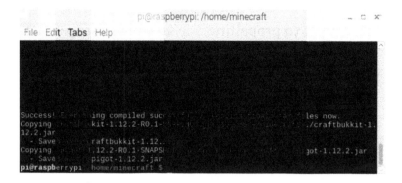

Have persistence and return following 60 minutes. In the event that all things go well you will have a record in your Minecraft organizer called nozzle 1.12.2.jar (or whatever the most recent adaptation is at the time).

4. Launching the Minecraft Server

It's a great opportunity to dispatch the server. Use ls direction to discover the spigot.jar document and it's variant.

There is ought to be record with a filename like nozzle [version].jar. At the hour of composing, this was nozzle 1.12.2.jar.

Step1:- Launch the server with the accompanying direction, ensure you enter the right form number.

sudo java -Xms512M -Xmx1008M -jar / home/minecraft/spigot-   [version].jar nogui

Subsequent to propelling, the server will stop conse-
quently (first time just) to affirm the permit under-
standing.

Step2:- Open the end-client permit agreement(EULA)
document utilizing this direction:

sudo nano eula.txt

Acknowledge the EULA by changing False to True, at
that point press Ctrl > X to exit and spare.

Step3:- Next, dispatch the server again utilizing a
similar order:

```
sudo java -Xms512M -Xmx1008M -jar /home/minecraft/spigot-[version].jar nogui
```

It will require some investment, as guide is building. It will take about thirty minutes, so show restraint

5. Connect to the Raspberry Pi Minecraft Server

Presently, your Minecraft server is online on your neighborhood arrange. You should simply dispatch Minecraft on your PC, at that point click Play > Servers - > Add server fill the new server subtleties, give it a name, and include the IP address.

You can discover the IP address of your server by composing following directions in the terminal:

sudo hostname -I

Presently, select the server to begin playing.

In the event that you have another Raspberry Pi, at that point you can play in that moreover. Raspberry Pi has inbuilt Minecraft game. Along these lines, you can associate this neighborhood minecraft with our recently made Minecraft server:

1. Open the Minecraft pi in the Game alternative.

2. Start the game on the server Raspberry Pi.

3. Snap on Join game in another raspberry pi and afterward your server IP will be shown, click on it. Presently, you can make the most of your game individually terms.

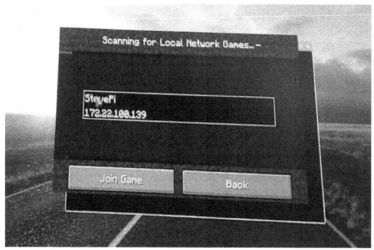

6. Configure Your Minecraft Server

In case you have tried the server and it is working effectively on your Rasbperry pi PC, at that point presently it's an ideal opportunity to arrange it. You need to alter server properties. Utilize the underneath direction to set the properties, it is a book record.

sudo nano /home/minecraft/server.properties

Anything you are evolving here, remember that Raspberry pi is certainly not a fast processor in this way, set the properties which requires less preparing. A run

down of server properties can be found on this connection Minecraft wiki .

At long last after all the arrangement and setup, you can alternatively introduce a module to counteract utilizing an excessive amount of RAM of Raspberry pi by Minecraft game. You need to introduce the No-SpawnChunks module to avert high RAM utilization by the Minecraft server.

In the first place, open the modules subdirectory by utilizing this order:

```
cd /home/minecraft/plugins
```

Download the NoSpawnChunks.jar document:

```
sudo wget -O NoSpawnChunks.jar http://
ci.dmulloy2.net/job/NoSpawnChunks/
```

Presently you have your very own Minecraft server which you can alter as per you. So now appreciate the game with your loved ones.